NATIONAL GEOGRAPHIC KIDS

T0010103

weird but true!

SHARKS

NATIONAL
GEOGRAPHIC
KIDS
That's weird!

weird
but
true!
SHARKS
300
FIN-NOMENAL
FACTS TO DIVE INTO
NATIONAL GEOGRAPHIC
WASHINGTON, D.C.

In the 16th century, sailors referred to sharks as sea dogs.
Ahoy, matey!
Shark egg cases are also known as mermaid purses.

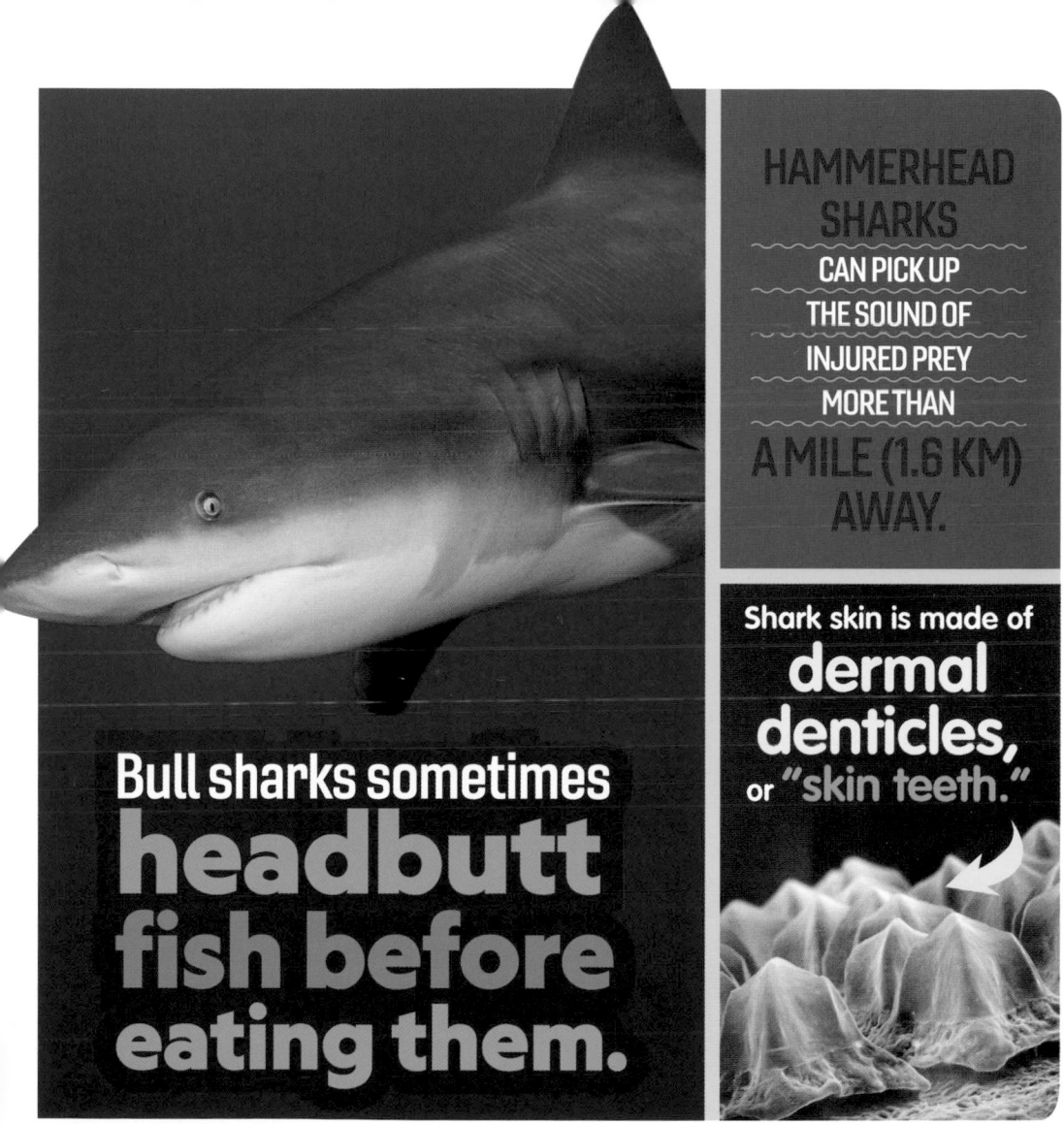
HAMMERHEAD SHARKS CAN PICK UP THE SOUND OF INJURED PREY MORE THAN A MILE (1.6 KM) AWAY.
Bull sharks sometimes headbutt fish before eating them.
Shark skin is made of dermal denticles, or "skin teeth."

A whale shark's SPOT PATTERN

is as UNIQUE as
a HUMAN'S
FINGERPRINT.

A POD OF ORCAS WILL SOMETIMES ATTACK A GREAT WHITE SHARK AND EAT ONLY ITS LIVER.

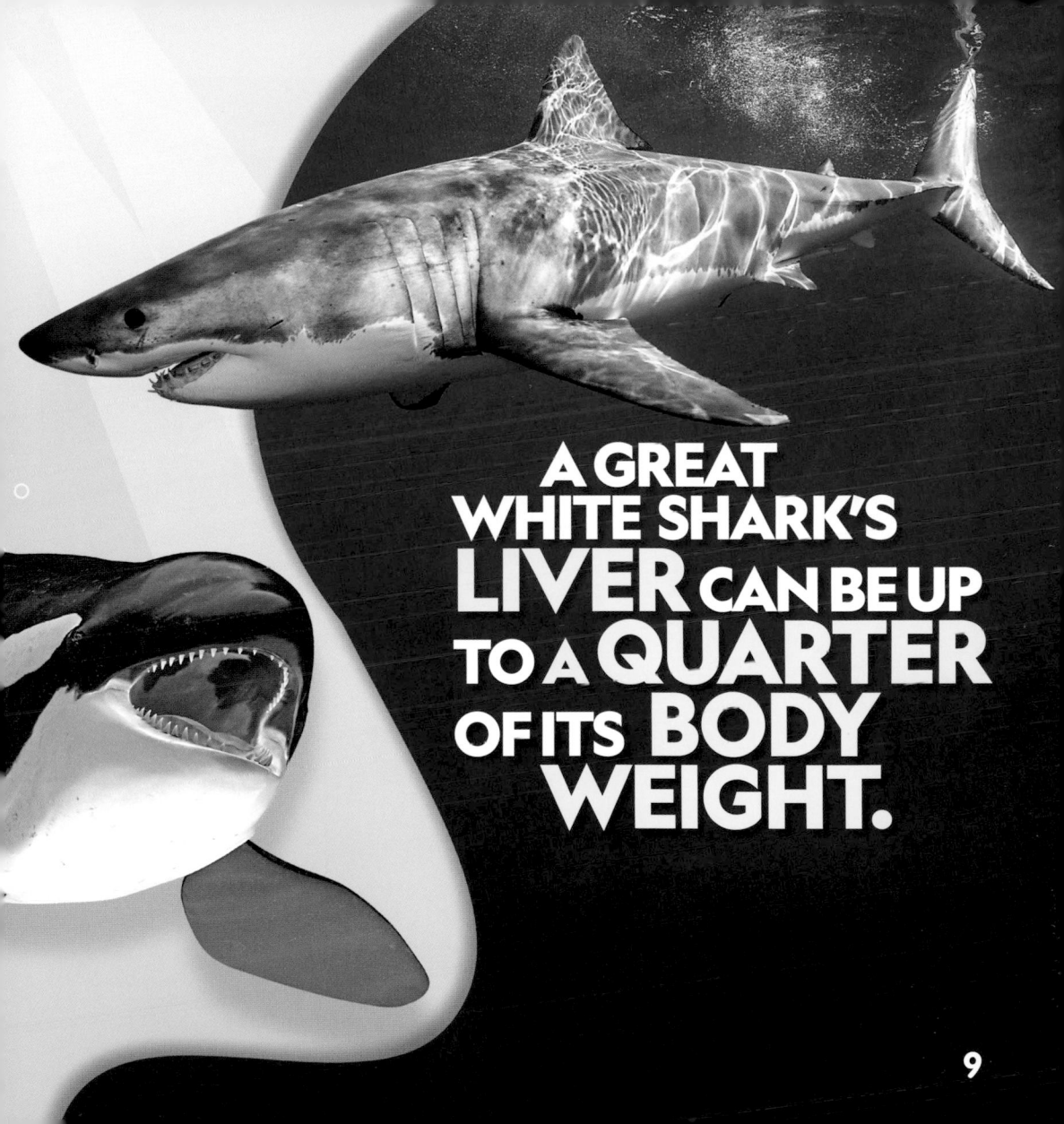

A GREAT WHITE SHARK'S LIVER CAN BE UP TO A QUARTER OF ITS BODY WEIGHT.

Edestus, an extinct prehistoric shark, sliced through prey with scissorlike jaws.

A Port Jackson shark mother screws her SPIRAL-SHAPED EGG CASE into rocks with her MOUTH.
The black TENDRILS that hang from the egg case get TANGLED IN SEAWEED to anchor it further.

WALKING SHARKS use their fins to **WALK ON THE SEAFLOOR** and even briefly **ABOVE WATER** on coral reefs.

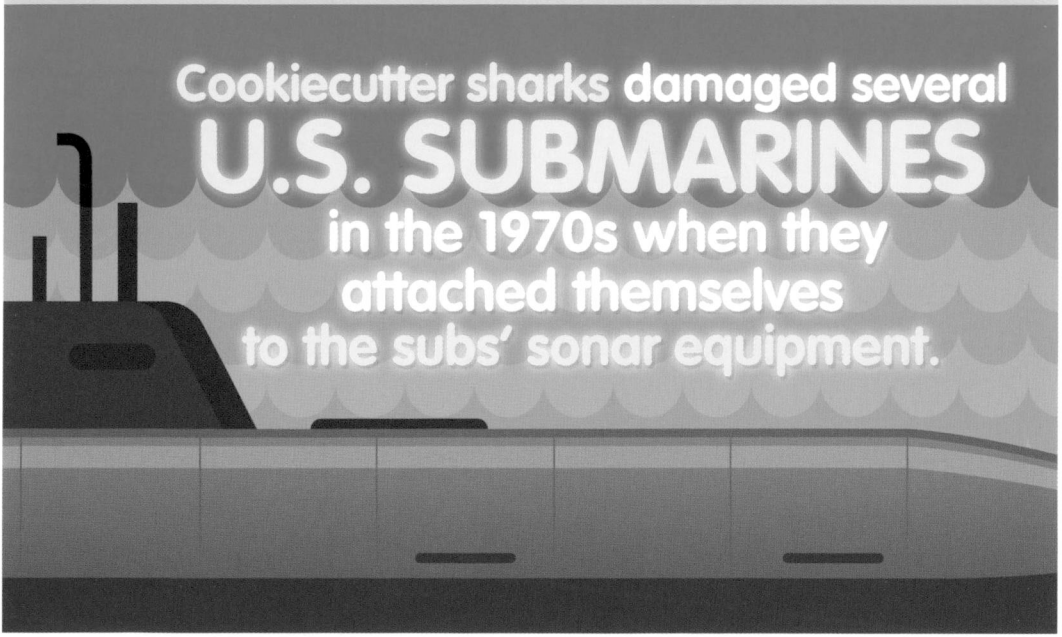

Cookiecutter sharks damaged several **U.S. SUBMARINES** in the 1970s when they attached themselves to the subs' sonar equipment.

A hammerhead shark's **nostrils,** just like **its eyes,** are located on either side of **its head.**

PYJAMA SHARKS
ARE NAMED FOR THEIR
STRIPED BODIES
THAT LOOK LIKE PJ'S.

Sharks don't blink.

More than
half of a
bonnethead
shark's diet
is seagrass.

Cookiecutter sharks use their sharp teeth to attach themselves to their prey and cut out a cookie-shaped chunk of flesh.

Only about **5 PERCENT** of shark species can live in **FRESHWATER.**

VIPER DOGFISH, A TYPE OF DEEP-SEA SHARK, USE THEIR EXTENDABLE JAWS TO **SNATCH PREY.**

Female sharks can have skin that is **two times thicker** than **male sharks'.**

Glowing with a blueish light, six-foot (1.8-m)-long **KITEFIN SHARKS** are the largest known **BIOLUMINESCENT VERTEBRATE.**

Part of a shark's intestines are CORKSCREW-SHAPED.

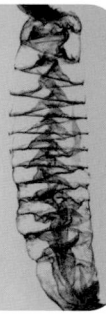

Greenland sharks sometimes eat land animals like horses and reindeer that fall through the ice into the ocean.

Greenland sharks TYPICALLY SWIM AT SPEEDS OF LESS THAN TWO MILES AN HOUR (3.2 KM/H).

Gray reef sharks form friendships that can last for years.

Hammerheads use their **hammer-shaped heads** to pin stingrays to the **ocean floor** before **eating them.**

SAW SHARKS HAVE SAWLIKE SNOUTS, WHICH THEY USE TO SLASH AT PREY.

PARASITES attach to and feed on **GREENLAND SHARKS' EYES,** leaving many of them with **POOR VISION.**

In the Middle Ages, **FOSSILIZED SHARK TEETH** were believed to be hardened **DRAGON OR SNAKE TONGUES.**

WOBBEGONG SHARKS
lie still on the ocean floor and then SUCK UP PASSING PREY whole with their VACUUM-LIKE MOUTHS.

BEARD-LIKE LOBES
around their mouths
help lure fish and
CRUSTACEANS.

Whitetip reef sharks poke their heads into coral reef crevices and snatch SLEEPING OCTOPUSES.
z-z-z

In 2012,
researchers studied
A 10-FOOT
(3-m)-LONG
female bull shark
nicknamed BIG BLUE
that weighed
about as much as a
GRAND PIANO.

TIGER SHARKS HAVE SERRATED TEETH THAT CAN CUT THROUGH TURTLE SHELLS.

EACH SCALE on a shark's skin is about **THE SAME WIDTH AS A FEW HUMAN HAIRS.**

LEOPARD SHARKS **SUCK OUT innkeeper worms** FROM THEIR BURROWS **to eat them.**

The sharks have been found with **bite marks from the worms** inside their mouths.

A female whale shark can give birth to as many as **300 pups.**

Bonnethead sharks use
EARTH'S MAGNETIC
FIELD to NAVIGATE.

Peter Benchley, the author of the 1974 novel **JAWS**, has a species of shark named after him: ***Etmopterus benchleyi.***

MOST SHARKS CAN SEE IN COLOR.

Porbeagles, a type of mackerel shark, **play—they roll in kelp** and **push floating objects.**

Porbeagle sharks have been seen **chasing each** other in what looks like **a game of tag.**

PACIFIC OCEAN
NORTH AMERICA
ASIA
INDIAN OCEAN
AUSTRALIA
OCEANIA
PACIFIC OCEAN
SOUTH AMERICA
0 2,000 miles
0 2,000 kilometers
MAP KEY
Size of Europe*
Size of shark sanctuaries in the Pacific Ocean
*Europe is placed on top of the shark sanctuaries to show the size comparision. This isn't the location of the continent.
Shark sanctuaries in the Pacific Ocean cover an area that is TWO TIMES THE SIZE OF EUROPE.
Some sharks grow a new set of teeth EVERY TWO WEEKS.

Scientists discovered that **tiger sharks** often prey on migrating land-based **songbirds** that fall in the sea during storms.

Sand sharks gulp air at the **ocean's surface** and then hold it in their stomachs, which lets them float **motionless** while they wait for prey.

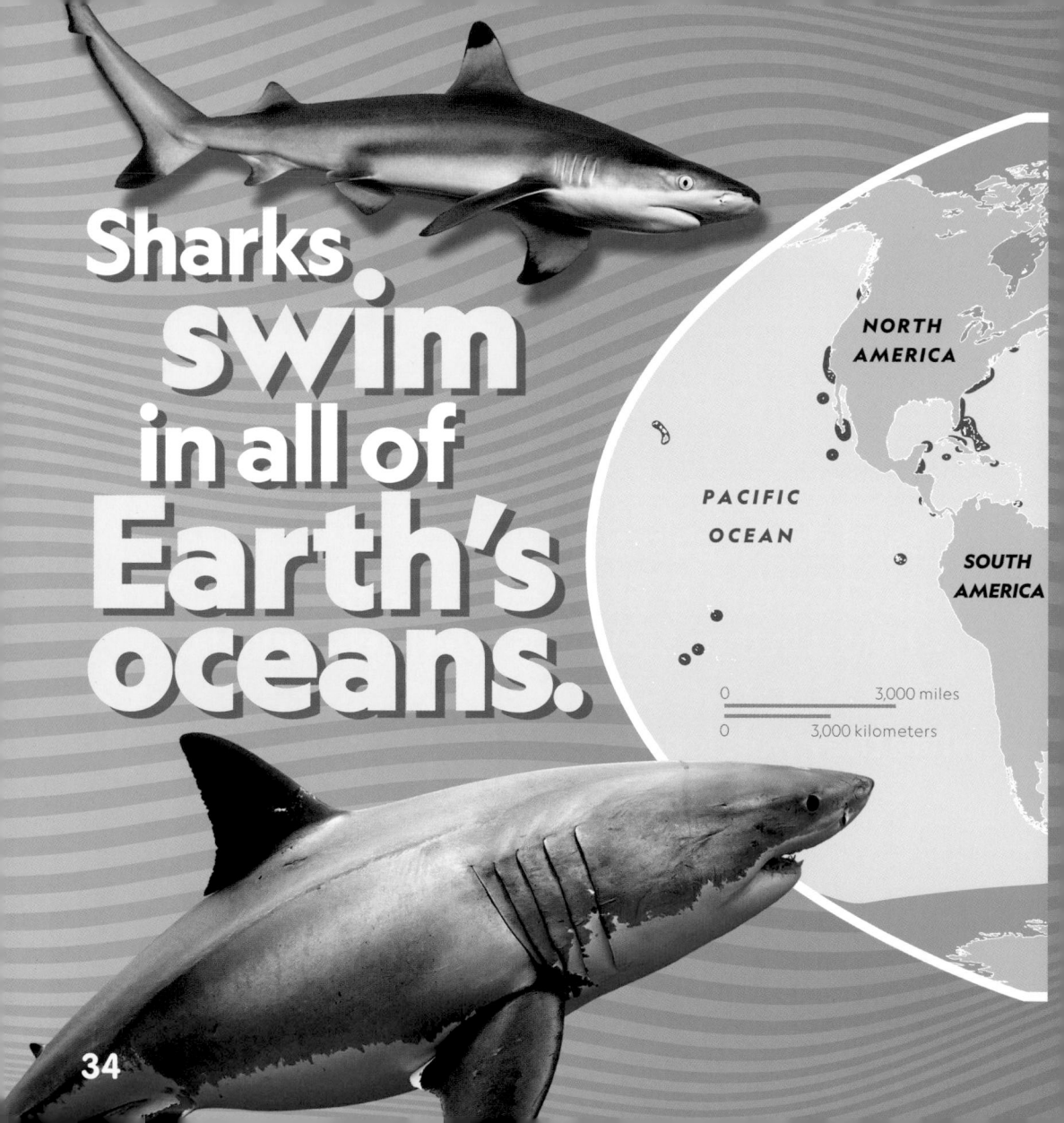
Sharks swim in all of Earth's oceans.
NORTH AMERICA
PACIFIC OCEAN
SOUTH AMERICA
0 3,000 miles
0 3,000 kilometers

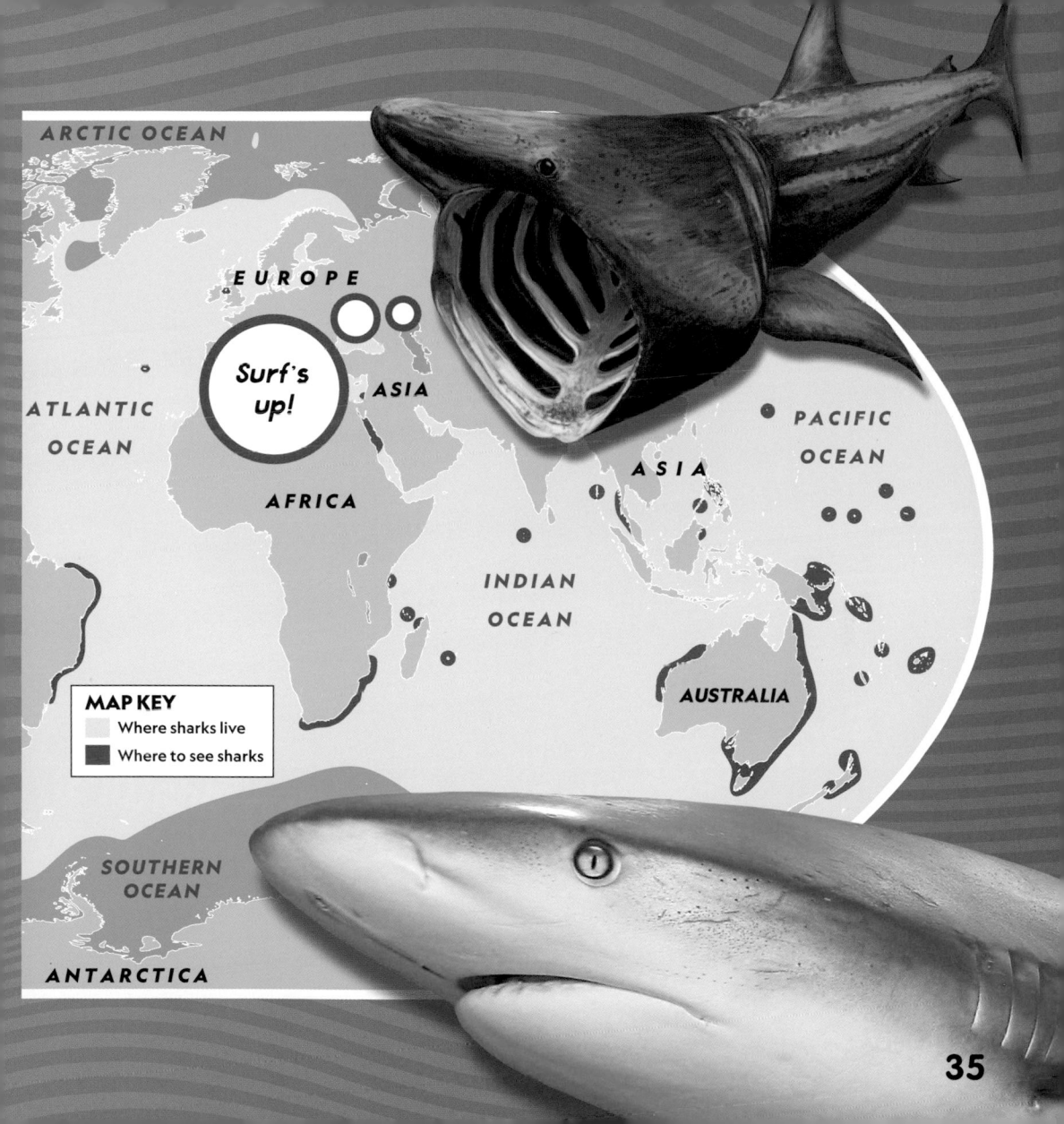
ARCTIC OCEAN
EUROPE
Surf's up!
ASIA
ATLANTIC OCEAN
AFRICA
PACIFIC OCEAN
ASIA
INDIAN OCEAN
AUSTRALIA
MAP KEY
Where sharks live
Where to see sharks
SOUTHERN OCEAN
ANTARCTICA

Great white sharks have only two predators:
orcas and humans

SCIENTISTS FOUND TAPEWORM EGGS IN **270-MILLION-**YEAR-OLD FOSSILIZED

SHARK POOP.

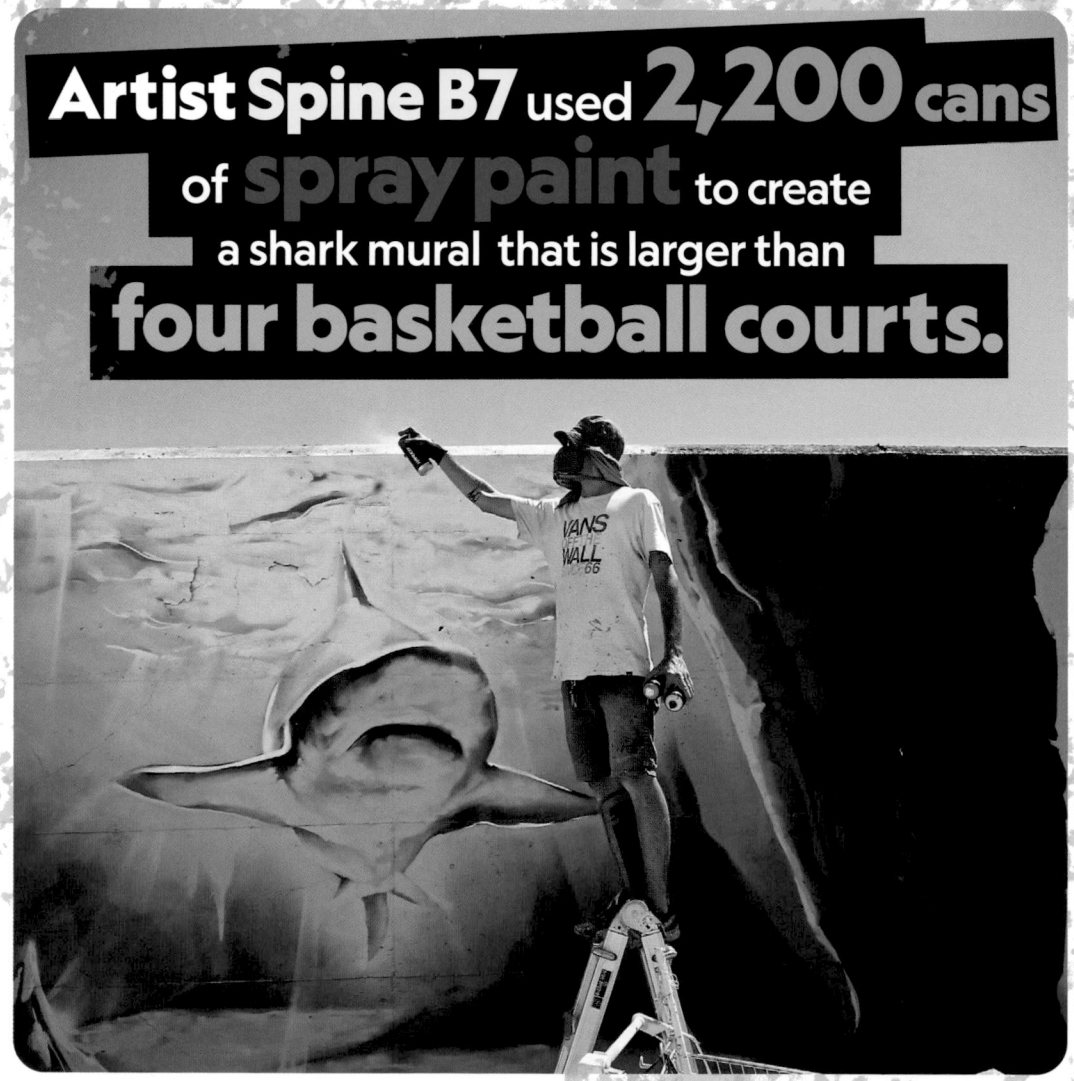
Artist Spine B7 used 2,200 cans
of spray paint to create
a shark mural that is larger than
four basketball courts.

Sharks survived
ALL FIVE OF
EARTH'S
MASS
EXTINCTIONS.
That's weird!

Sharks find food using

SPECIAL PORES ON THEIR SNOUTS,

which sense the electrical currents their prey give off.

Great white sharks **CHOMP** **their prey,** then shake it from side to side to **tear the flesh loose.**

SAND TIGER PUPS EAT EACH OTHER WHILE INSIDE THEIR MOTHER'S WOMB, LEAVING ONLY ONE PUP TO BE BORN.

A few fossilized scales from 450 million years ago are the earliest evidence of sharklike animals.

Remora fish have a *suction cup-like* structure on *top of their heads* that help them *cling to sharks.*

When a shark finds something to eat, the remora **detaches itself** to **snack on the leftovers.**

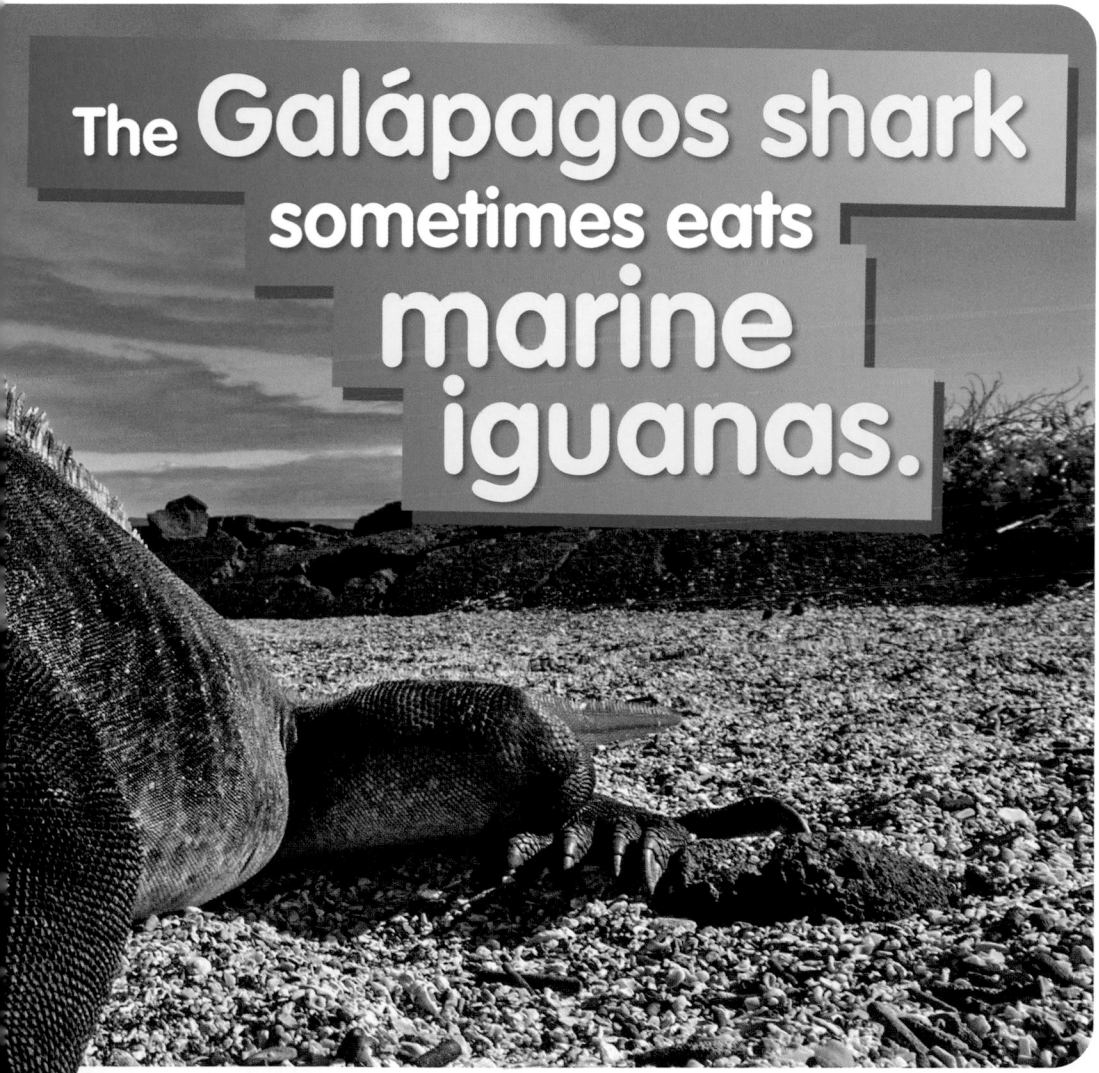
The Galápagos shark
sometimes eats
marine
iguanas.

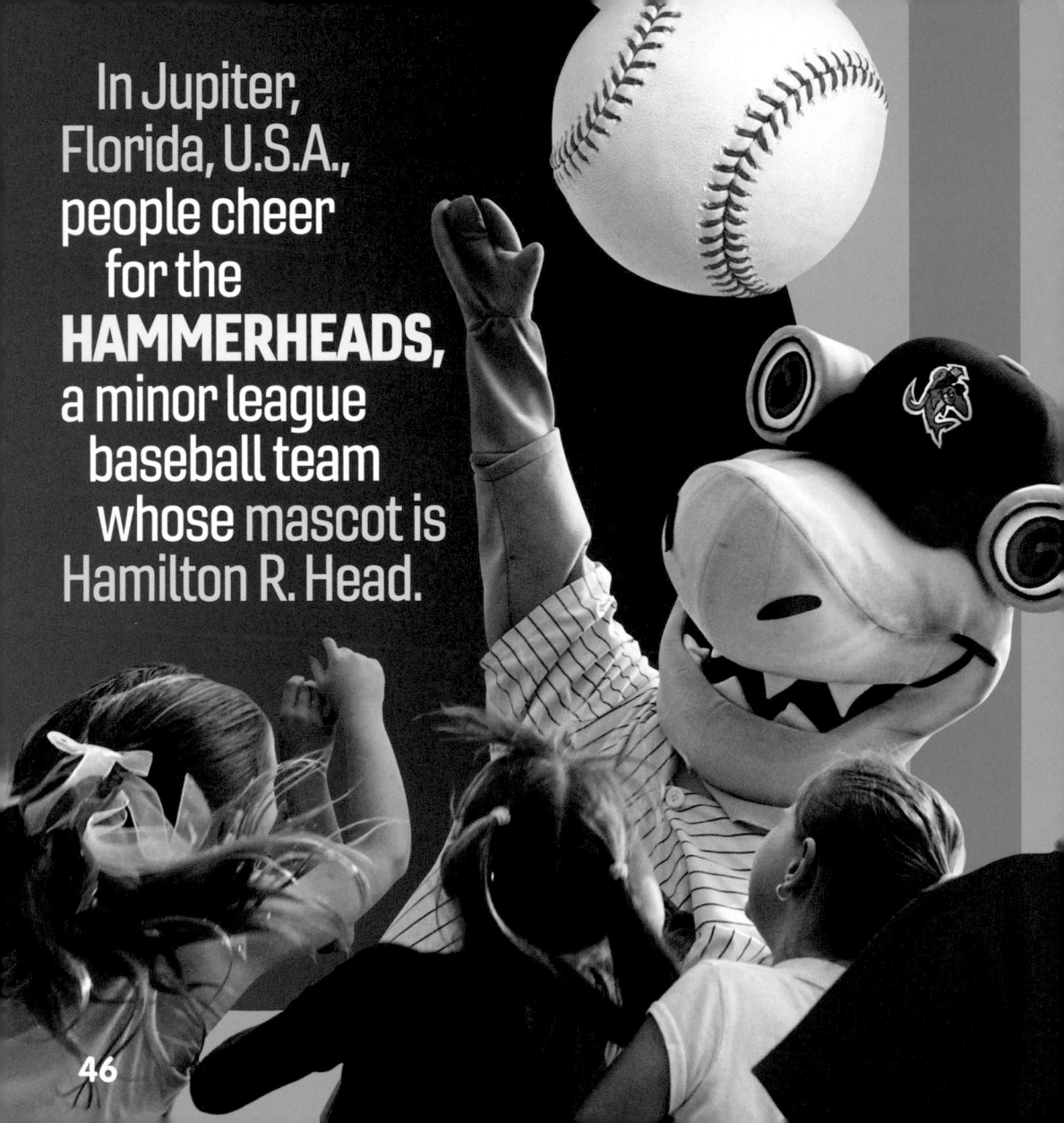

In Jupiter, Florida, U.S.A., people cheer for the **HAMMERHEADS,** a minor league baseball team whose mascot is Hamilton R. Head.

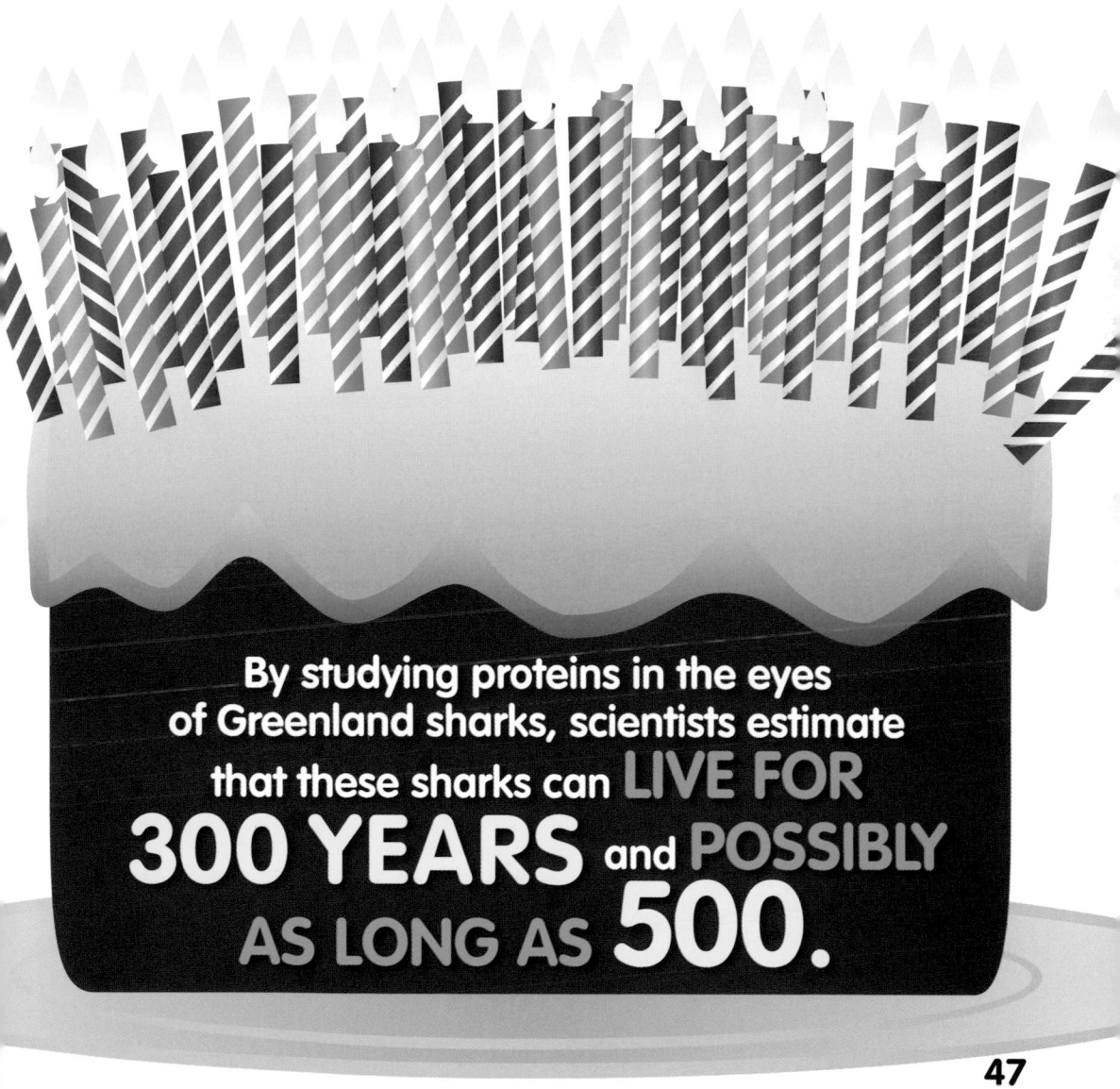
By studying proteins in the eyes of Greenland sharks, scientists estimate that these sharks can LIVE FOR 300 YEARS and POSSIBLY AS LONG AS 500.

The largest fish is **THE WHALE SHARK.**

If a shark is **turned over on its back,** it goes into **a relaxed, trancelike state.**

There are more than **500 species** of shark.

MEGAMOUTH SHARKS
migrate every day:
They leave shallow water to
follow plankton,
their prey, to the deep sea
AT SUNSET.

The "Baby Shark" video has been viewed more than 11 billion times.
The Washington Nationals went on a winning streak after outfielder Gerardo Parra chose it as his walk-up song in 2019.

Lemon shark skin looks YELLOW in shallow water, where these sharks live.

JULY 14 is SHARK AWARENESS DAY.

Frilled sharks have 25 rows of backward-facing, trident-shaped teeth.

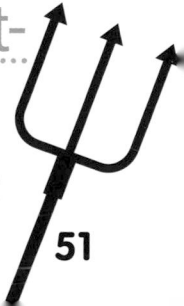

Scientists have spotted
fewer than
50 GOBLIN
SHARKS
in the ocean.

FAST-SWIMMING
SHORTFIN MAKOS
ARE NICKNAMED
"BLUE DYNAMITES."

In 2012, an inflatable shark nicknamed CHOMPIE "SWAM" through a building in Silver Spring, Maryland, U.S.A.

That's weird!

Scientists have seen seals blow bubbles in kelp forests to confuse sharks.

Megalodon ate 2,500 pounds (1,134 kg) of food a day—

BASKING SHARK MOMS
GIVE BIRTH TO PUPS THAT ARE
TALLER THAN
THE AVERAGE
14-YEAR-
OLD.
that's like you eating more than 20,000 hot dogs!

One of the earliest sharks, *Xenacanthus*, looked like an eel.

Scientists found that
BABY LEMON SHARKS
have DISTINCT PERSONALITIES:
Some are STANDOFFISH,
and others are
OUTGOING.
You be you.

The prehistoric male ***Stethacanthus*** had a fin on its back shaped like an **ironing board.**

Some **unborn sharks** can sense danger and **stop moving in their egg case** so that predators don't **detect them.**

SHORTFIN MAKO SHARKS CROSS UP TO 2,485 MILES (4,000 KM) OF OCEAN DURING THEIR ANNUAL MIGRATIONS.

One man from Utah, U.S.A., has collected more than 800 rubber sharks.

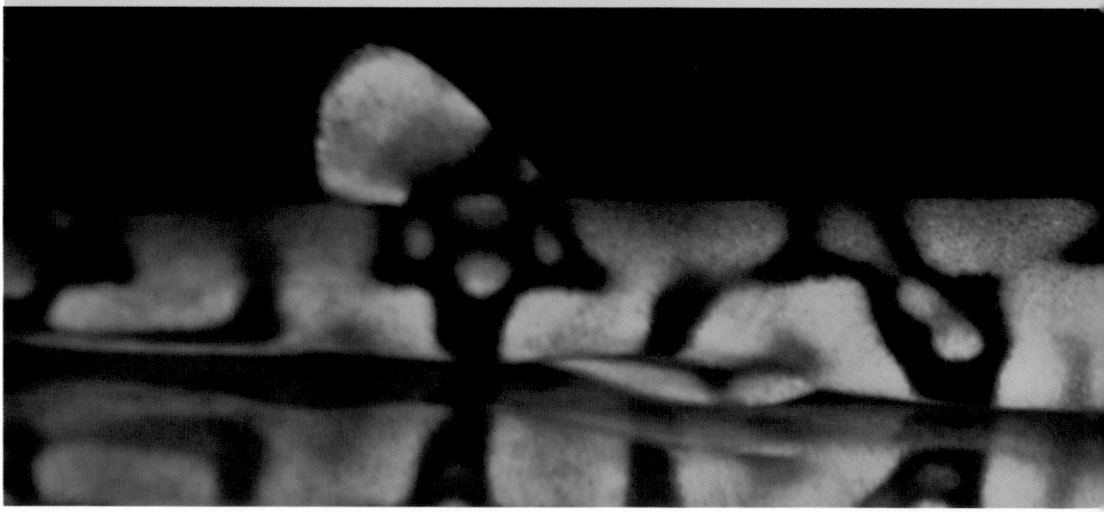

A marine robot called the WasteShark can gobble up about 16 tons (14.5 t) of trash from the ocean each year.

Cat sharks give off a GREENISH LIGHT to COMMUNICATE with each other, but it's invisible to HUMANS.

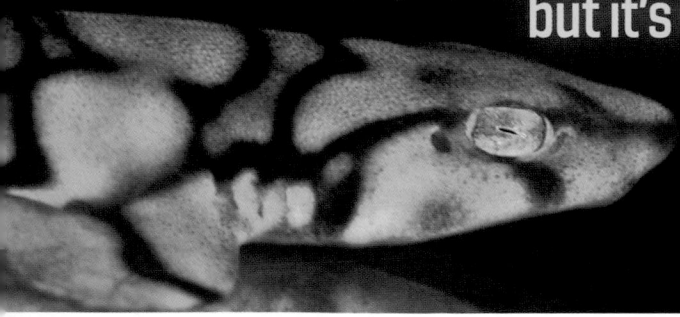

Red sea urchins, the main diet of horn sharks, stain the sharks' teeth reddish brown.

Sharks use their inner ears to keep their balance—just like we do.

The basking shark's common name comes from how it stays at the water's surface to BASK, or SOAK, in the SUN.

SHORTFIN MAKO SHARKS, the fastest sharks on Earth, chase prey in short bursts at **35 miles an hour** (56 km/h).

OCEANIC WHITETIP SHARKS swim through SCHOOLS OF TUNA WITH OPEN MOUTHS, waiting for FISH TO SWIM INSIDE.

Nurse sharks partially

bury themselves in the sand

and breathe through openings behind their eyes.

"White Shark Café" is a large area in the Pacific Ocean where great white sharks migrate in the fall to feast.

Horn sharks' spines turn **PURPLE** when they eat a lot of purple sea urchins.

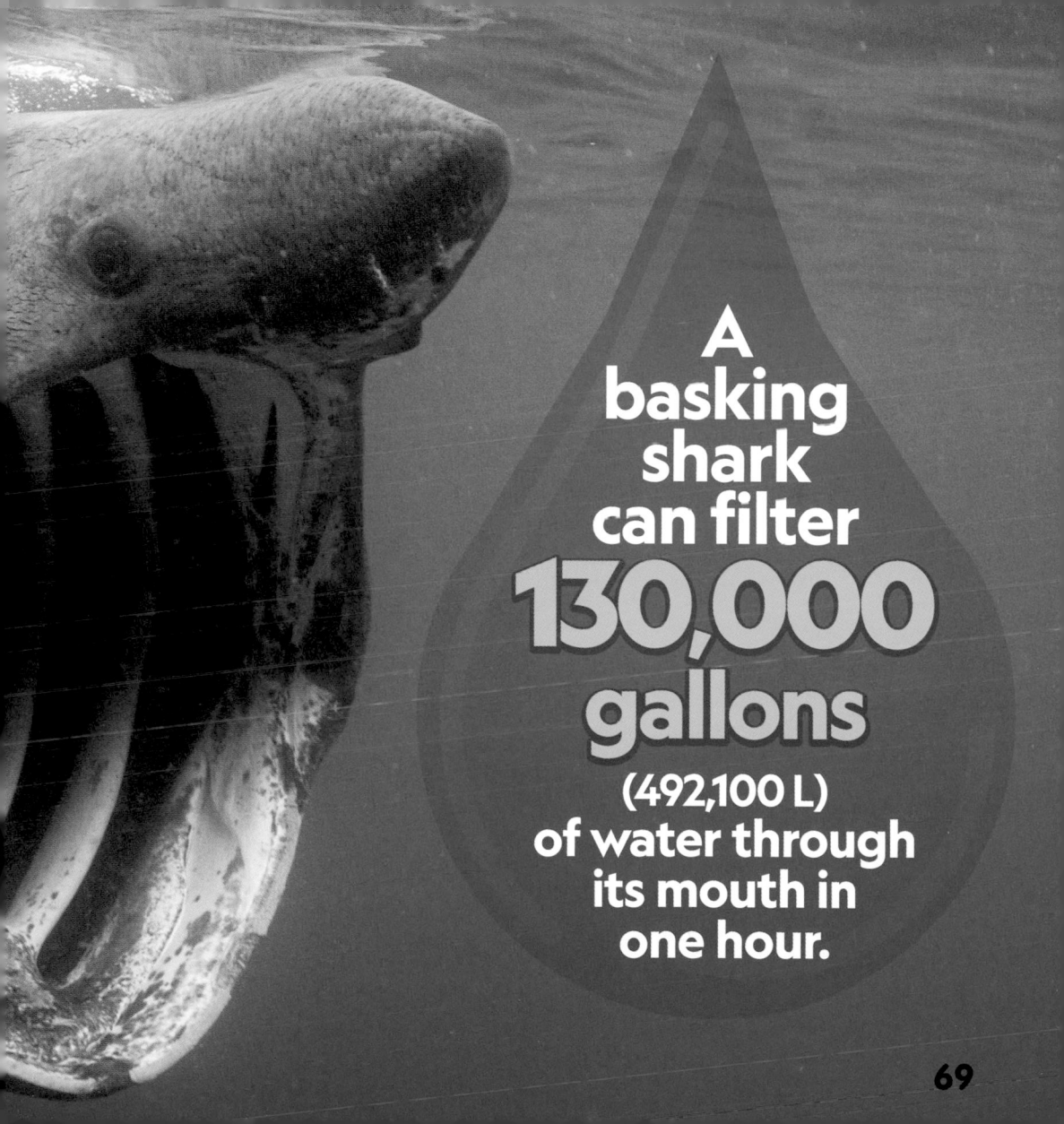
A basking shark can filter
130,000 gallons
(492,100 L)
of water through its mouth in one hour.

SCIENTISTS HAVE FOUND FOSSILIZED CROCODILE POOP WITH SHARK TEETH MARKS IN IT.
The extinct megalodon was almost three times longer than a great white shark.

A shark's jaws aren't attached to its skull, allowing it to **THRUST ITS MOUTH FORWARD WHEN ATTACKING.**

Riders on the **Leap of Faith waterslides** in the Bahamas and Dubai shoot through **A CLEAR TUBE** surrounded by sharks.

CROCODILE SHARKS repeatedly **SNAP THEIR JAWS** open and closed if **TAKEN OUT OF THE WATER.**

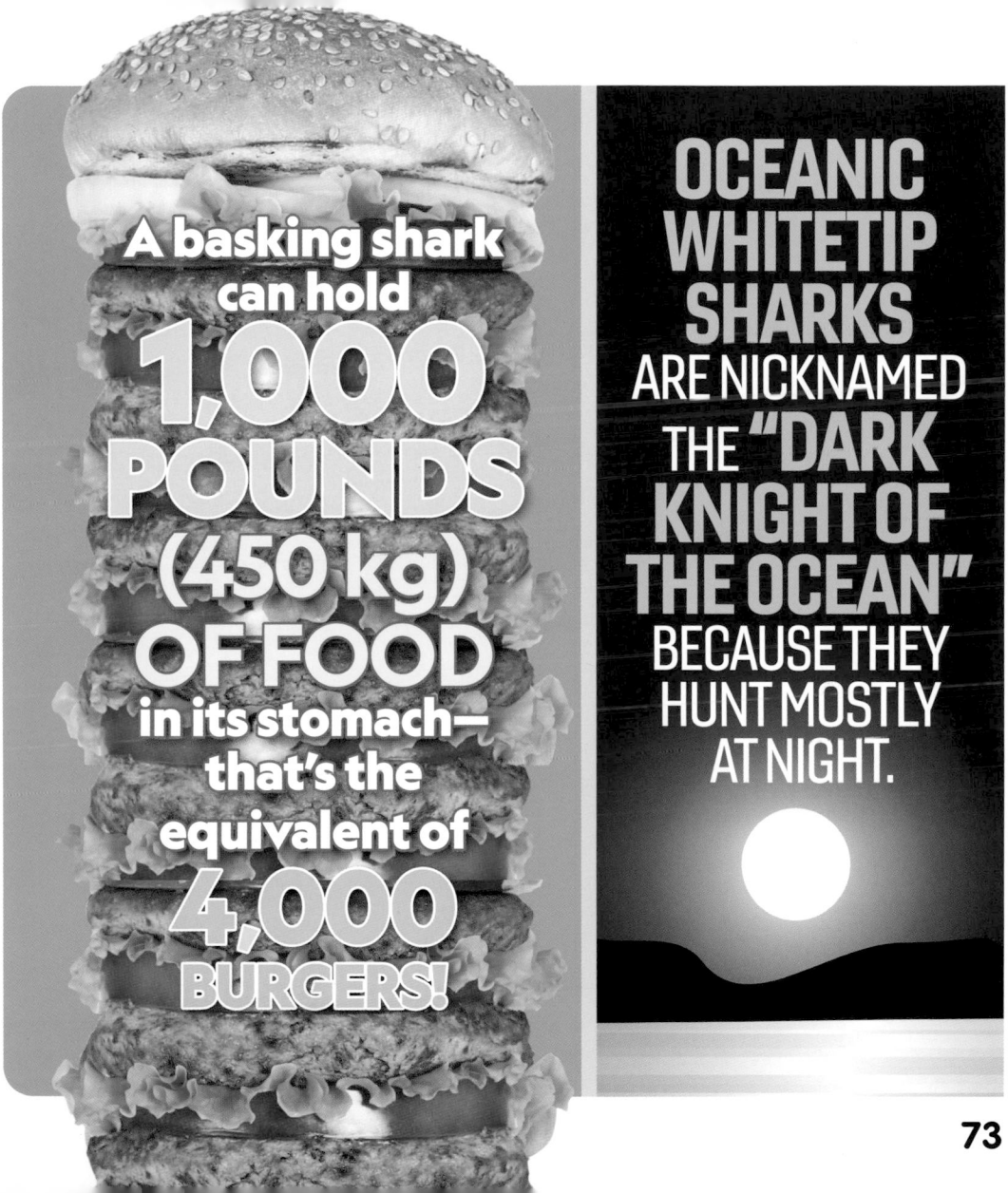
A basking shark can hold
1,000 POUNDS (450 kg) OF FOOD
in its stomach—that's the equivalent of
4,000 BURGERS!
OCEANIC WHITETIP SHARKS
ARE NICKNAMED THE "DARK KNIGHT OF THE OCEAN"
BECAUSE THEY HUNT MOSTLY AT NIGHT.

In the movie Jaws,
hidden scuba divers
sometimes steered
the full-scale
models of
the great white shark.

The crew collectively
nicknamed the trio of
mechanical sharks BRUCE.

Galápagos sharks arch their backs
and swim in figure eights to try to intimidate predators.
When pyjama sharks attack, they bite and then twist their prey's body in a maneuver called a
death roll.

Sharks' **TEXTURED SKIN** makes them **RESISTANT** to barnacles and algae.

The United States Navy studied shark skin to make a material that **KEEPS BARNACLES** from attaching to **SHIP HULLS.**

Galápagos fur seals **hunt less frequently during full moons,** likely because the light makes them more visible to sharks.

Goliath groupers prey on whitetip reef sharks, swallowing them whole.

Indigenous people in Brazil used shark teeth as **TOOLS,** which never had to be sharpened because shark teeth don't dull.

The state fossil of Georgia, U.S.A., is a **SHARK TOOTH.**

Researchers are studying
SHARKS' TAILS to make better
UNDERWATER VEHICLES.

Unlike other fish, sharks can **stiffen their tails mid-swish,** which creates twice as many **jets of water** and makes them **swim faster.**

SHARKS CAN **DETECT MOVEMENT IN COMPLETE DARKNESS.**

GREAT WHITE SHARKS CAN
LEAP OUT OF THE WATER
WHEN ATTACKING PREY.

One species of frilled shark has a dorsal fin that can look like a horse's mane.
A beachgoer has only a one in 11.5 million chance of being bitten by a shark.
Sharks spit out food they don't like.

Caribbean reef sharks **pile on** top of one **another** in caves, lying completely still for hours.

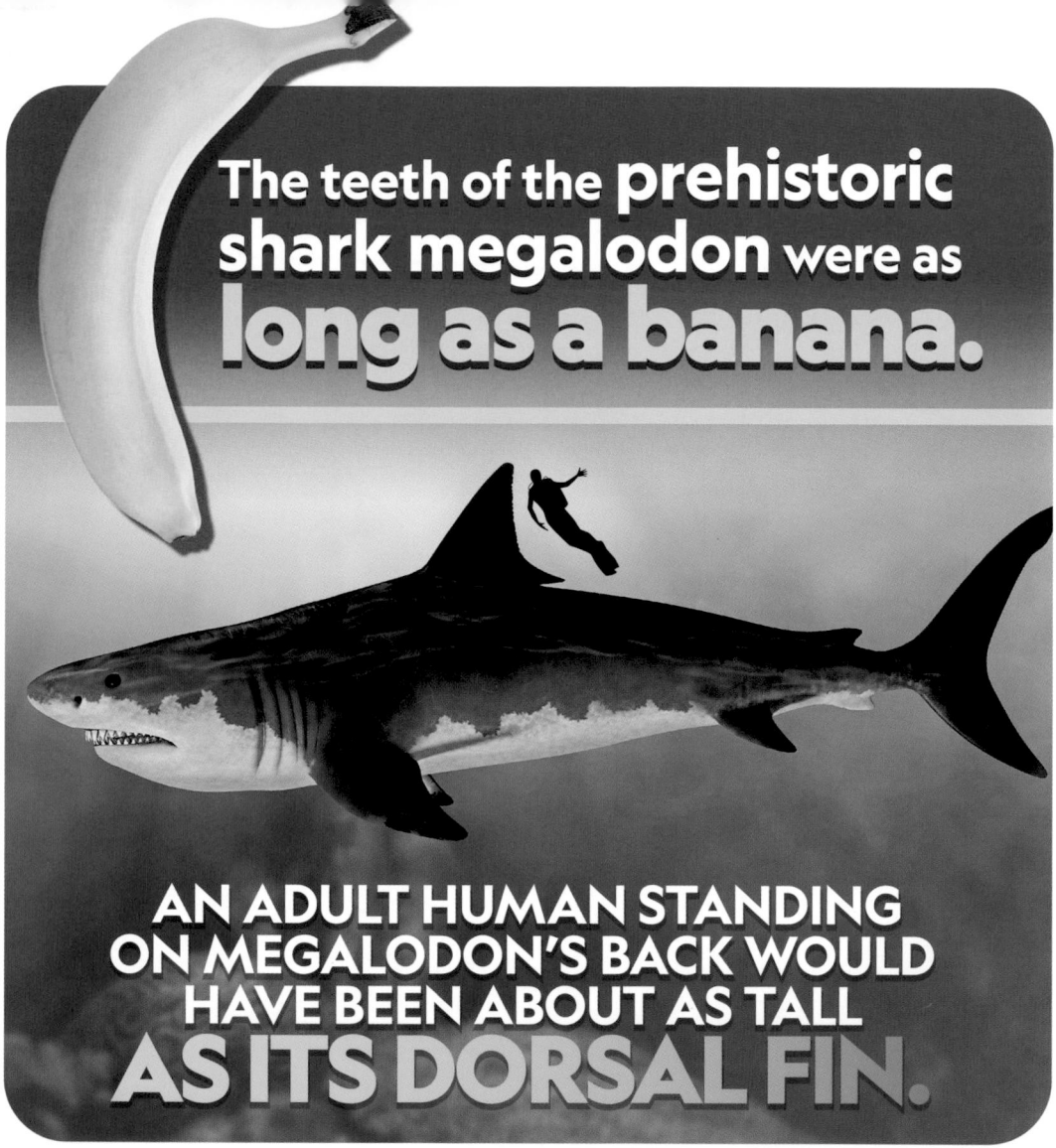
The teeth of the prehistoric shark megalodon were as long as a banana.
AN ADULT HUMAN STANDING ON MEGALODON'S BACK WOULD HAVE BEEN ABOUT AS TALL AS ITS DORSAL FIN.

FEMALE GREENLAND SHARKS DON'T REPRODUCE UNTIL THEY ARE ABOUT 150 YEARS OLD.
I don't look a day over 149.

Bull sharks are rarely in aquarium exhibits—they'll eat the other fish.

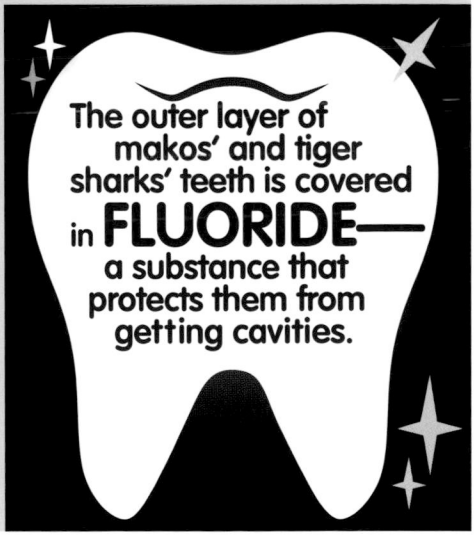
The outer layer of makos' and tiger sharks' teeth is covered in FLUORIDE—a substance that protects them from getting cavities.

SAW SHARKS are born with teeth that LIE FLAT AGAINST THEIR SNOUTS and later POP OUT to the sides.

AMERICAN ALLIGATORS sometimes attack LEMON, NURSE, and BONNETHEAD SHARKS.

BASKING SHARKS are sometimes called **elephant sharks** because of their **TRUNK-LIKE SNOUTS.**

In the movie
Finding Dory,
Destiny the whale shark
says she taught Dory to speak whale, but
whale sharks are sharks, **not whales.**

Cat sharks stay in their **egg cases for two years before emerging.**

Great white sharks can detect a single drop of blood in the water from up to a third of a mile (.53 km) away.

Sevengill sharks use **comb-shaped teeth** on their lower jaws to **grab hold of prey** and jagged teeth on their upper jaws to **saw off flesh.**

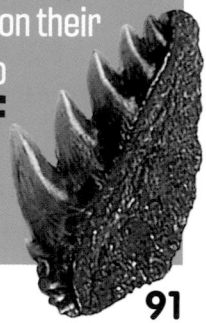

Bull sharks will **slowly swim around remoras** to let them know they can **eat parasites** from the sharks' mouths, gills, and bodies.

Sharks can't swim backward.

Angel sharks can snatch their prey in about one-tenth of a second.

ZEBRA SHARK PUPS ARE BORN WITH STRIPES THAT SLOWLY CHANGE TO DARK SPOTS.
Sharks can go more than a month without a big meal.

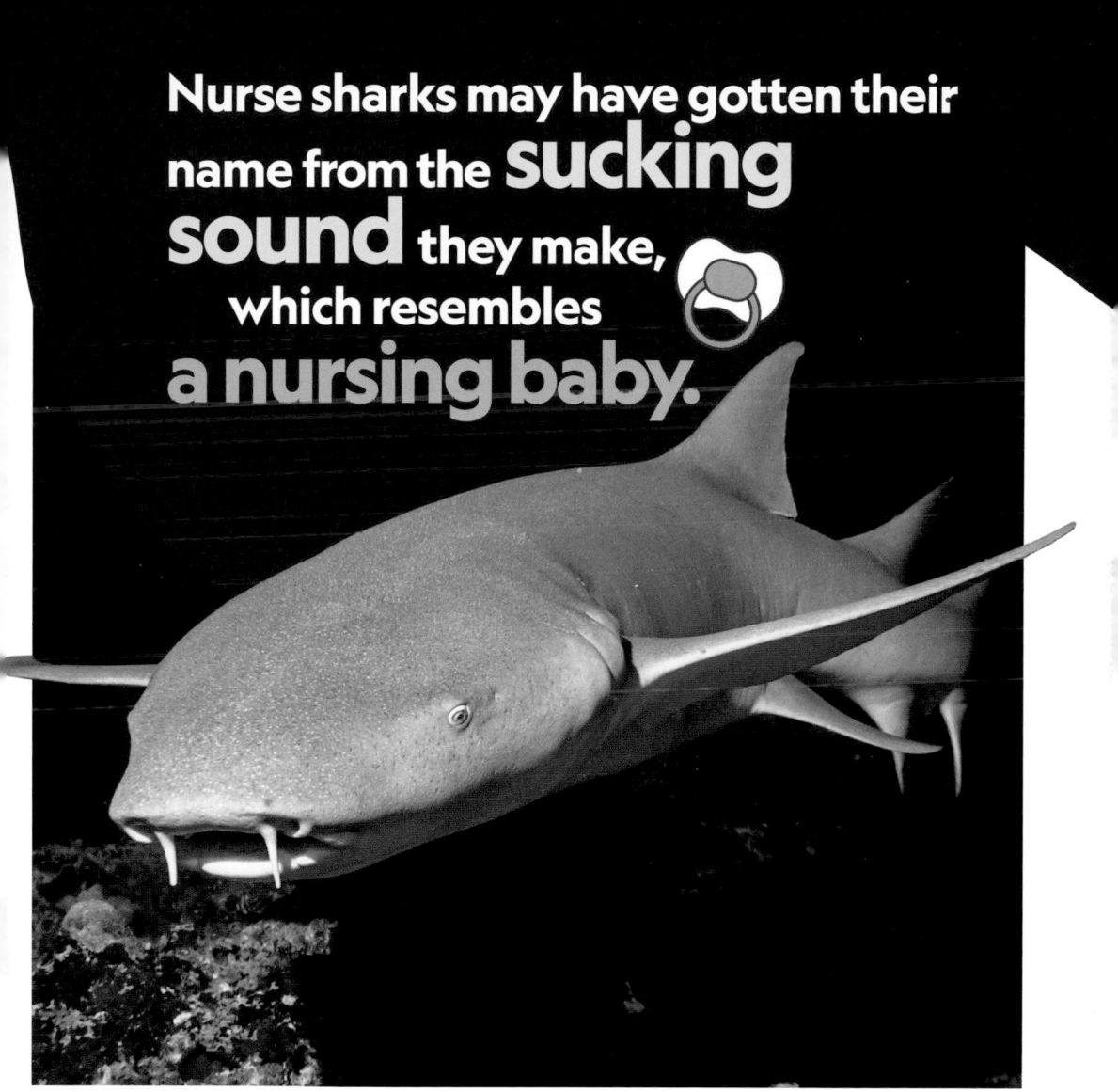
Nurse sharks may have gotten their name from the sucking sound they make, which resembles a nursing baby.

Some sharks can go through
40,000
TEETH
in their lifetime.

To identify an individual whale shark by its unique pattern of spots, scientists use software that NASA developed to map the stars.

During the Middle Ages, people thought shark tooth fossils could DETECT POISONS.

THE 300-MILLION-YEAR-OLD *ORTHACANTHUS* SHARK SOMETIMES ATE ITS OWN YOUNG.

SAWFISH—CLOSELY RELATED TO SHARKS—USE THEIR SAWLIKE JAWS TO RAKE THROUGH SAND TO FIND WORMS, SHRIMPS, AND CRABS TO EAT.

Some sharks push their stomachs out of their mouths to rinse them off.

Frilled sharks have **THICK SKIN FOLDS** along their bellies, which scientists think might **EXPAND TO HELP THEM DIGEST LARGER PREY.**

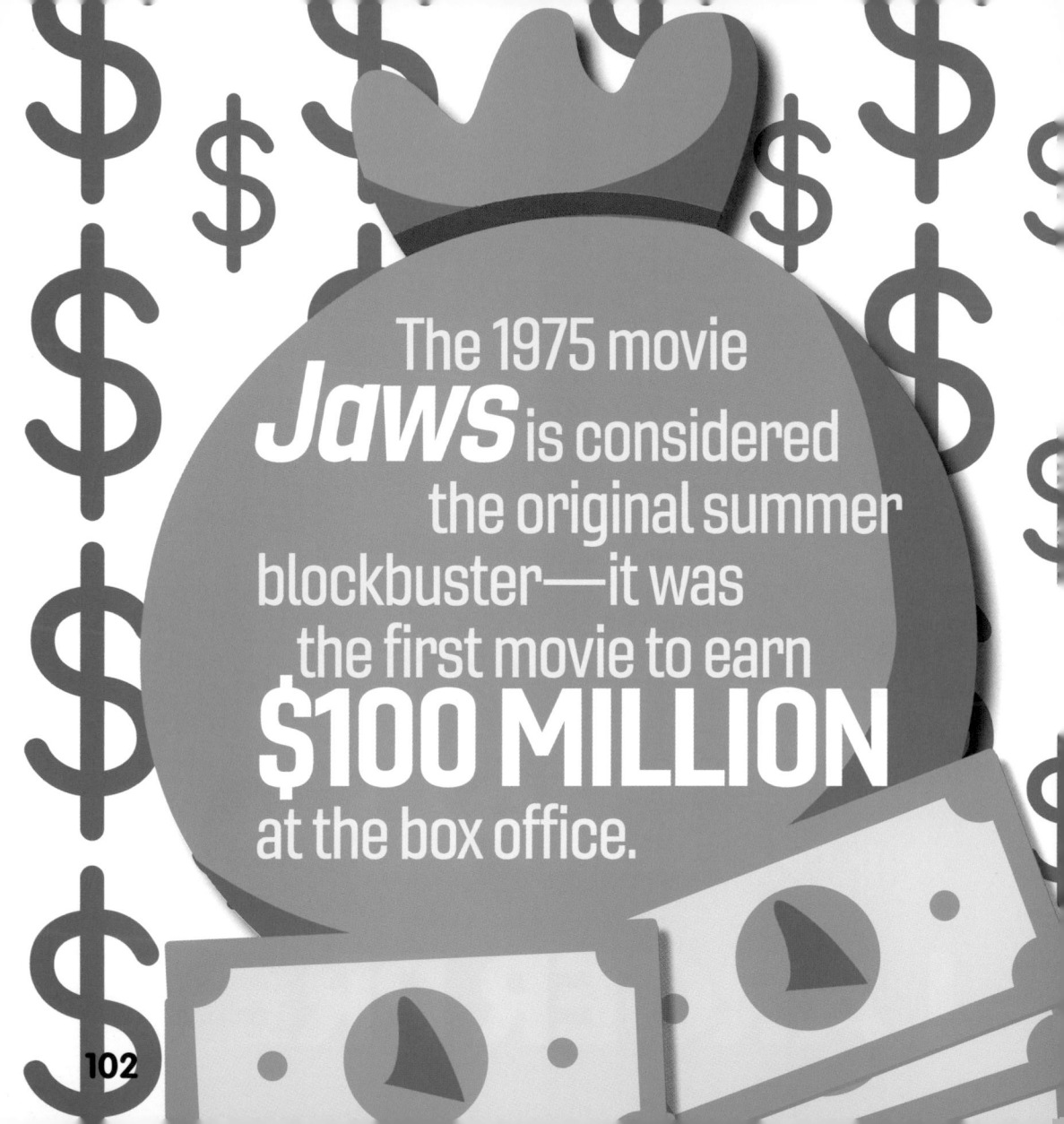
The 1975 movie
Jaws is considered
the original summer
blockbuster—it was
the first movie to earn
$100 MILLION
at the box office.

THREE ELITE MOUNTAIN CLIMBERS TOOK 12 DAYS TO CLIMB MERU PEAK IN INDIA BY SCALING A GRANITE WALL KNOWN AS SHARK'S FIN.

A 20-story apartment building SHAPED LIKE A SHARK FIN in Cancún, Mexico, includes a shark research lab.

Cape fur seals attack and eat BLUE SHARKS.

A sand tiger shark's teeth **STICK OUT** of its mouth even when it's closed.

Some shark poop is spiral-shaped.

A SHARK'S STOMACH CONTAINS **ACIDS** STRONG ENOUGH TO **DISSOLVE METAL.**

The ancient shark
SQUALICORAX snatched
dinosaurs and pterosaurs
that FELL INTO
THE WATER.

It takes shark teeth about
10,000 YEARS
to fossilize.

In 2020, the MONSTER TRUCK MEGALODON jumped over eight other Monster Jam trucks—A WORLD RECORD.

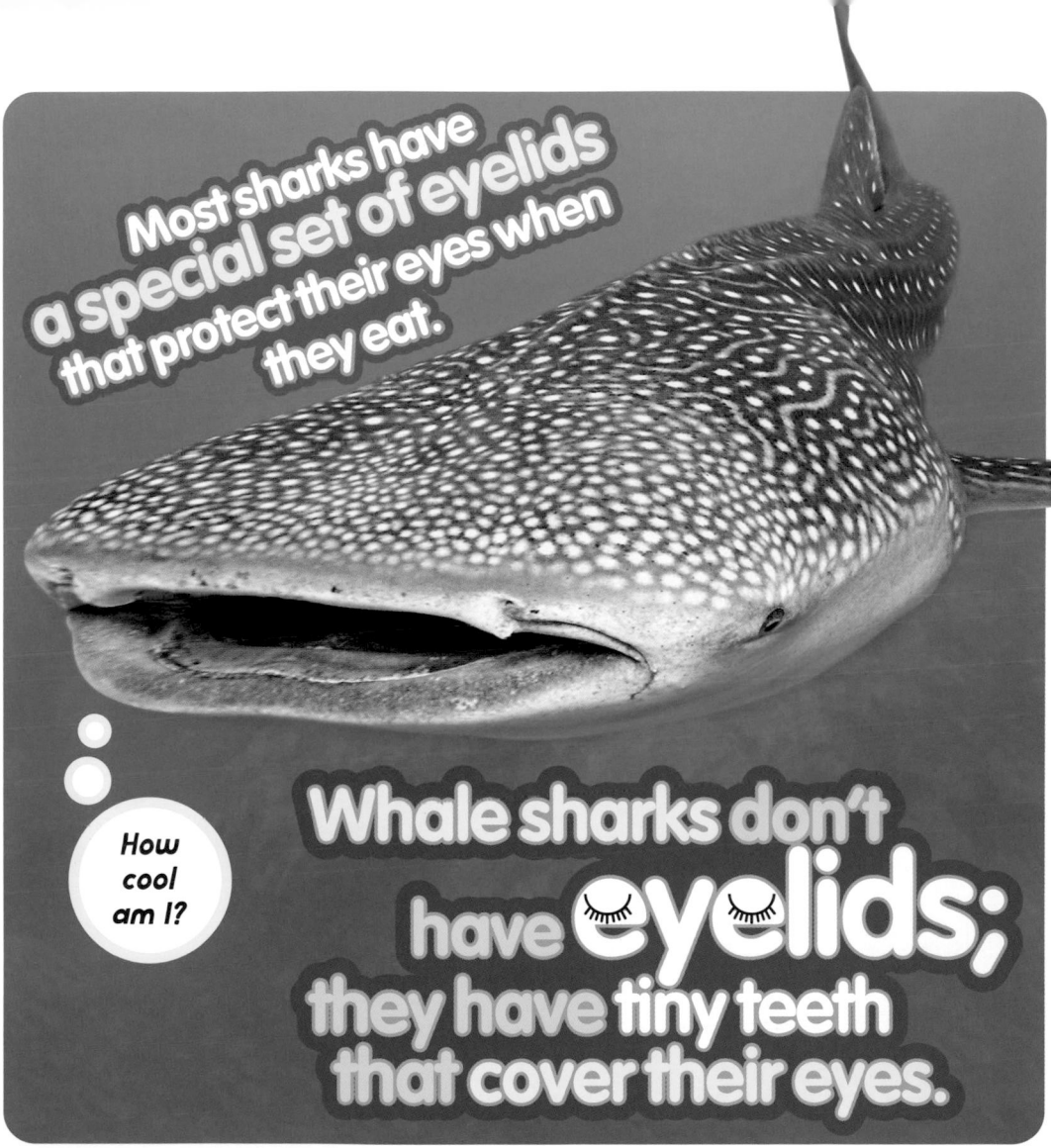
Most sharks have a special set of eyelids that protect their eyes when they eat.
How cool am I?
Whale sharks don't have eyelids; they have tiny teeth that cover their eyes.

The **NINJA LANTERNSHARK** emits **a faint glow** that allows it to blend in with the **OCEAN'S LOW LIGHT** and **sneak up on prey.**

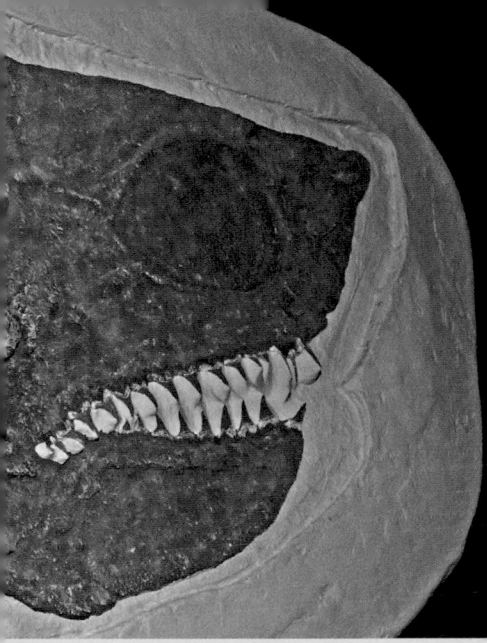

The **extinct "ginsu"** shark was nicknamed for a brand of **sharp chopping knives** after scientists found fossil evidence that it **sliced its prey into pieces.**

Its stealth moves inspired the **eight-year-old cousins** of the scientist who discovered the shark to come up with its **common name.**

USING **TRASH** FOUND **ON THE BEACH,** SUCH AS **BOTTLE CAPS, TOILET SEATS,** AND **TOYS,**

AN ARTIST CREATED **A GREAT WHITE SHARK SCULPTURE NAMED GRETA.**

Tiger sharks swim in
large loops
as they search for prey.
I'm getting dizzy...

You can use white modeling chocolate, sugar cubes, and marshmallows to make teeth for a shark cake.

The Smithsonian National Museum of Natural History has a FULL-SIZE MODEL of A FEMALE MEGALODON hanging in its café.

A newborn great white shark is as long as a bathtub.
A newborn whale shark is about as long as a skateboard.

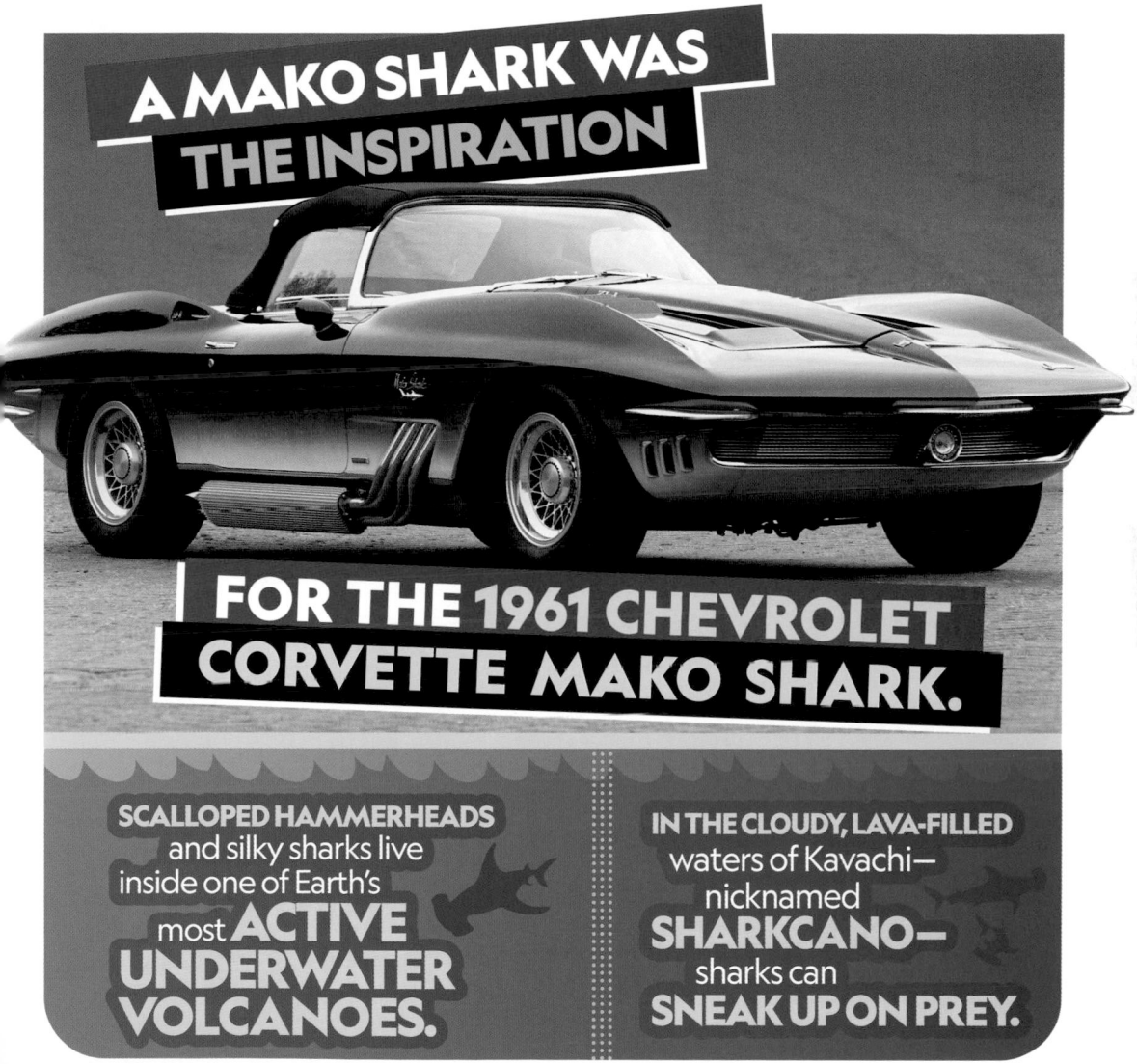
A MAKO SHARK WAS
THE INSPIRATION
FOR THE 1961 CHEVROLET
CORVETTE MAKO SHARK.
SCALLOPED HAMMERHEADS
and silky sharks live
inside one of Earth's
most ACTIVE
UNDERWATER
VOLCANOES.
IN THE CLOUDY, LAVA-FILLED
waters of Kavachi—
nicknamed
SHARKCANO—
sharks can
SNEAK UP ON PREY.

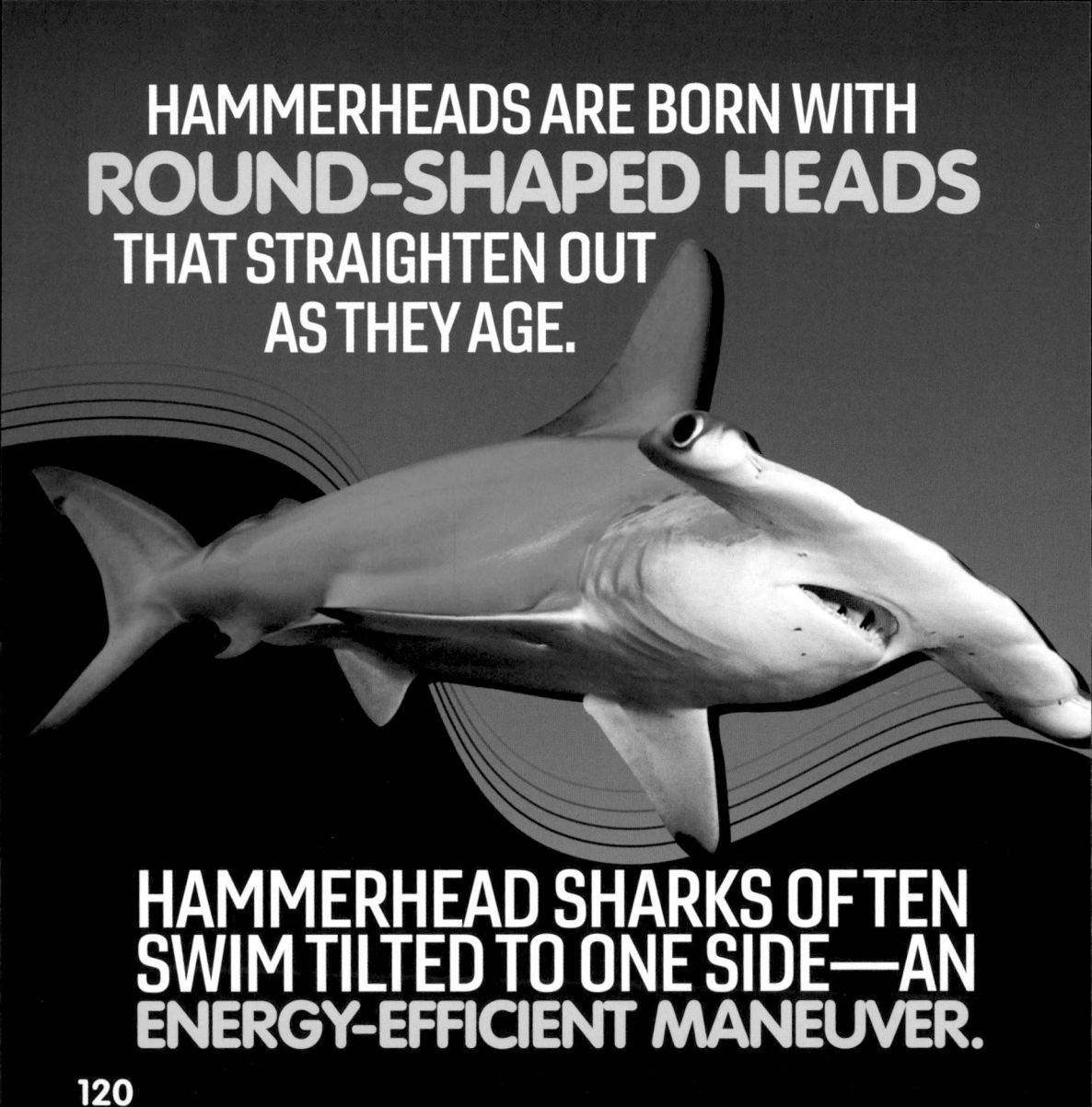

HAMMERHEADS ARE BORN WITH **ROUND-SHAPED HEADS** THAT STRAIGHTEN OUT AS THEY AGE.

HAMMERHEAD SHARKS OFTEN SWIM TILTED TO ONE SIDE—AN **ENERGY-EFFICIENT MANEUVER.**

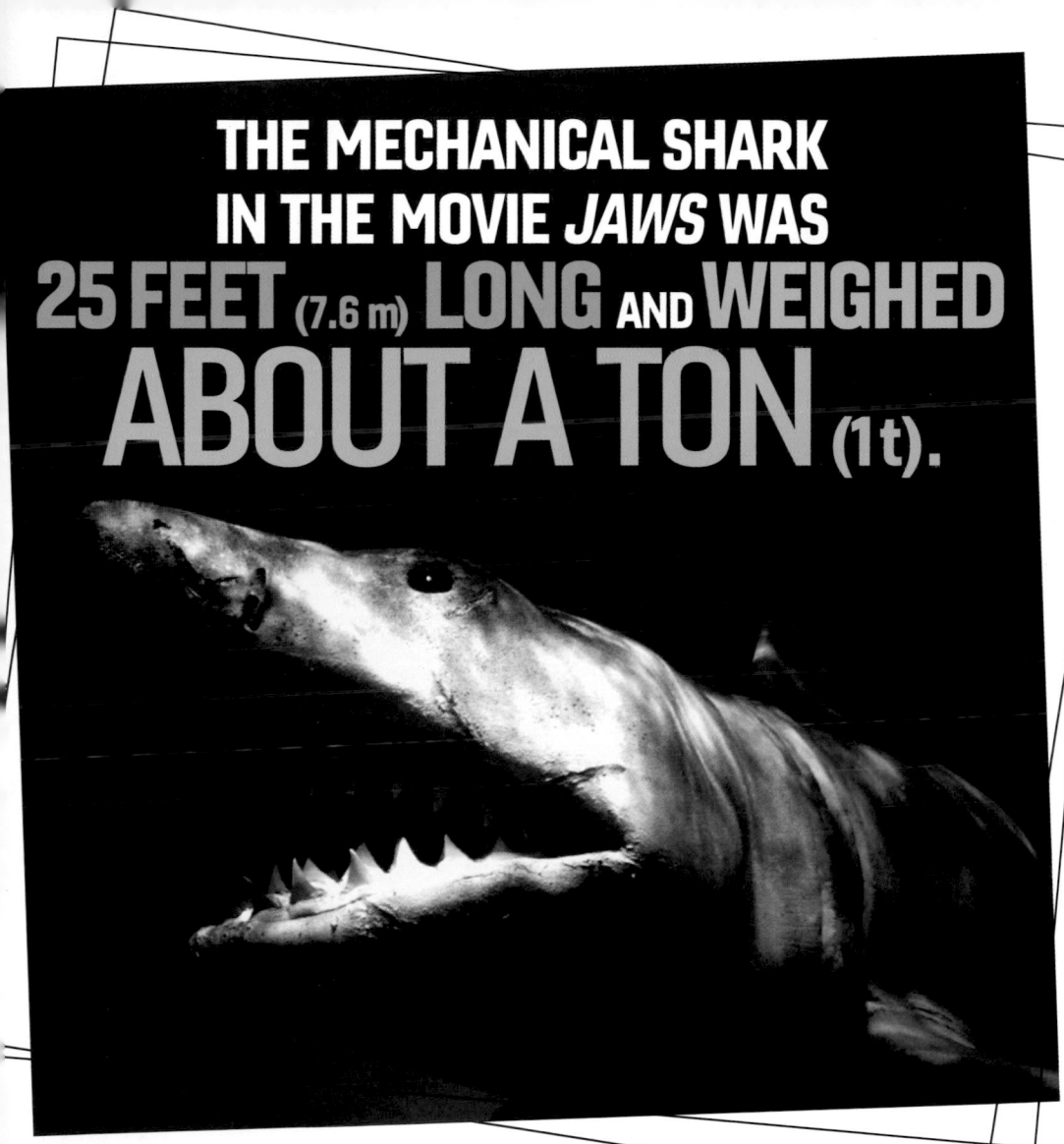

THE MECHANICAL SHARK IN THE MOVIE *JAWS* WAS 25 FEET (7.6 m) LONG AND WEIGHED ABOUT A TON (1 t).

Sharks that prey on large, fast-moving fish have bigger eyes than ones that hunt slow-moving animals.

PYGMY
RIBBONTAIL
CAT SHARKS
ARE ABOUT THE
LENGTH OF A
PIECE OF TOAST.

When people first settled in Iceland around A.D. 1000, they snacked on fermented Greenland sharks.

They made *hákarl,* or "rotten shark," by burying the sharks in sand for months.

The United States Navy once **issued a shark repellent** called **Shark Chaser** to pilots who might **crash-land in the sea.**

Shark Chaser was **a pink pill** that, when dropped in water, **released black ink** to **hide the pilots in the ocean.**

Cat sharks got their name from their catlike, ALMOND-shaped eyes.
Scientists think that sharks can see about 10 TIMES BETTER in LOW LIGHT THAN HUMANS.

HORN SHARKS HAVE A HORNLIKE RIDGE OVER EACH EYE.

GREAT WHITE SHARK ATTACKS ON HUMANS ARE OFTEN "SAMPLE BITES"—

the sharks release, rather than prey on, people.

When on the attack, salmon sharks swim in tight circles around schools
of their prey, Pacific salmon being one of their favorite foods.

Scientists think
that great whites
may be able to change
their skin color to camouflage
themselves from prey.

En garde!

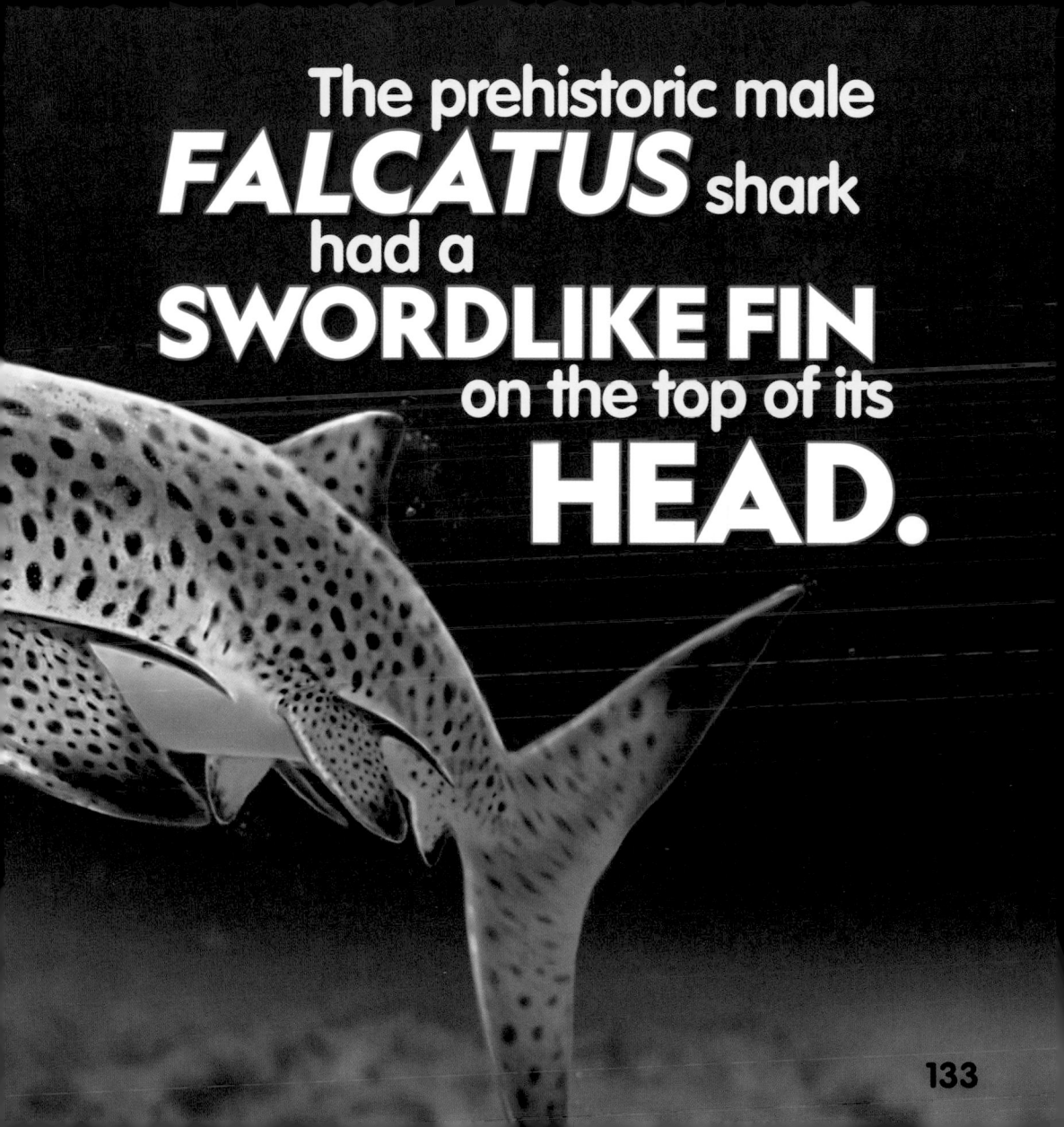

The prehistoric male **FALCATUS** shark had a **SWORDLIKE FIN** on the top of its **HEAD.**

ONLY THE UPPER TEETH
of the snaggletooth shark
have JAGGED EDGES,
which is why
its scientific
name means
"HALF SAW."

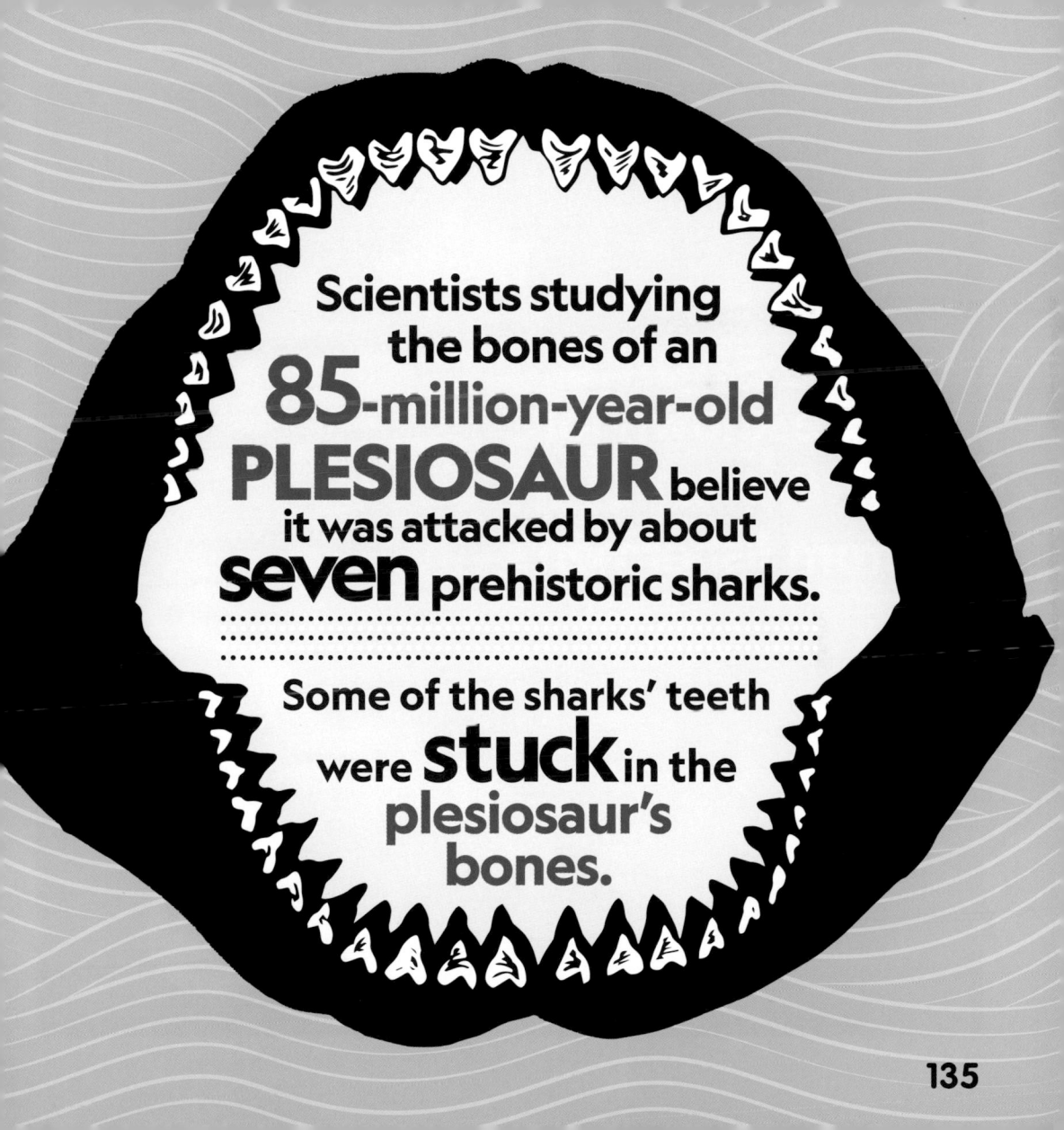
Scientists studying the bones of an 85-million-year-old PLESIOSAUR believe it was attacked by about seven prehistoric sharks.
Some of the sharks' teeth were stuck in the plesiosaur's bones.

Blue sharks are known for stealing fish from fishermen's nets.
Nothing to see here.

YOU CAN BUY A YOGA MAT DESIGNED TO MIMIC SHARK SKIN, WHICH PREVENTS BACTERIA FROM ATTACHING TO IT.

THE PREHISTORIC *PTYCHODUS* HAD TEETH SHAPED LIKE GARBAGE CAN LIDS THAT COULD CRUSH HARD-SHELLED PREY SUCH AS GIANT CLAMS.

PTYCHODUS IS KNOWN AS THE CRUSHER.

AT AN **ART GALLERY** IN MARATHON, FLORIDA, U.S.A., THERE ARE STAIRS THAT ALLOW VISITORS TO **CLIMB INSIDE NIBBLES THE SHARK'S HEAD.**

The frilled shark can **SWALLOW PREY HALF ITS SIZE.**

Fossilized shark teeth can be **WHITE, BROWN,** or **BLACK—** or even **BLUE.**

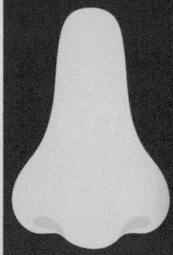

Sharks don't have **BONES;** their skeletons are made of **CARTILAGE,** the same material as your **EARS** and the tip of your **NOSE.**

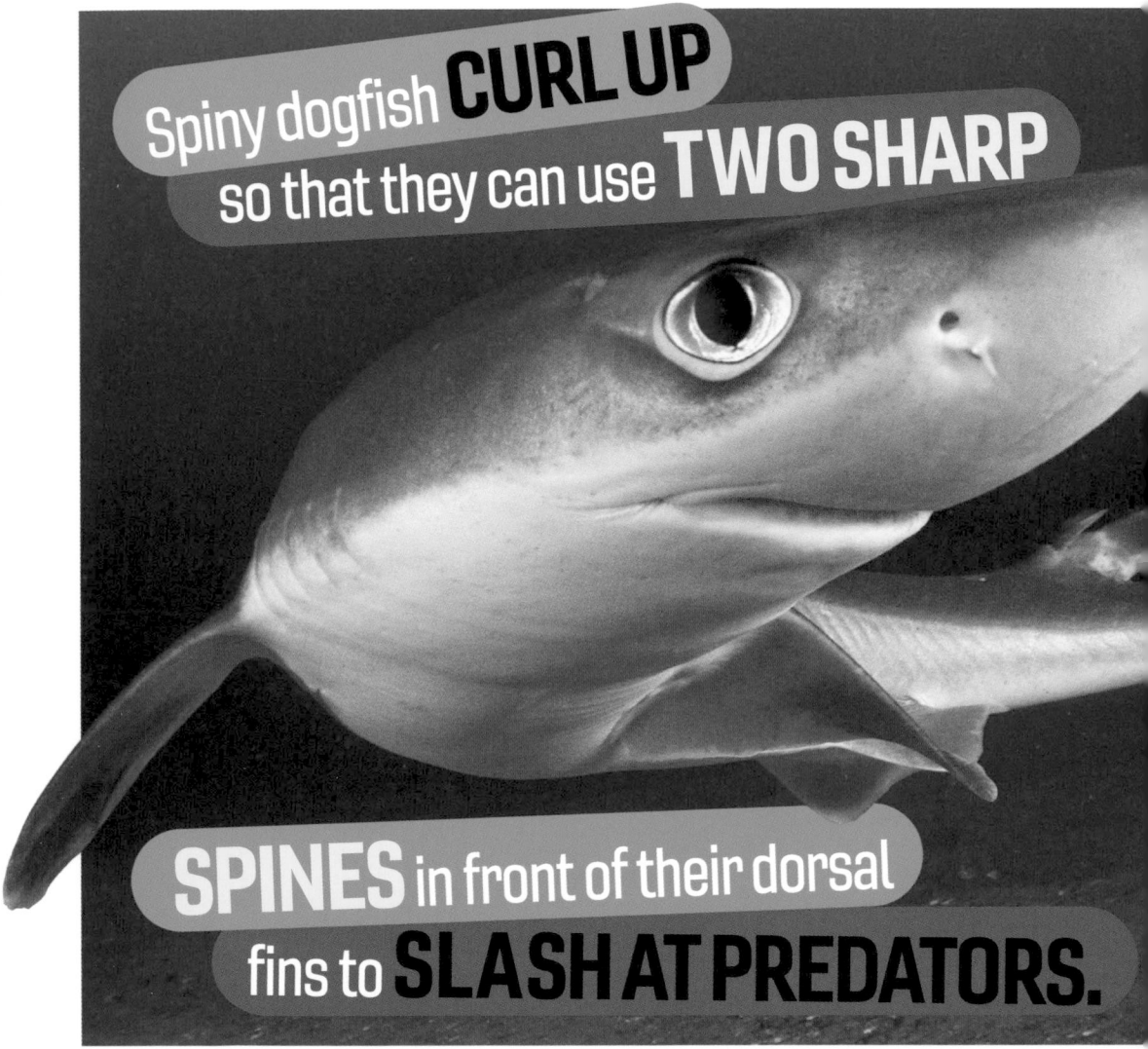
Spiny dogfish CURL UP
so that they can use TWO SHARP
SPINES in front of their dorsal
fins to SLASH AT PREDATORS.

The music that plays when the shark appears in *Jaws* consists of just two pairs of alternating notes—E and F or F and F sharp.

Divers swim in the **ICE-COVERED TOBOL RIVER** in Siberia to search for **FOSSILIZED SHARK TEETH.**

PYJAMA SHARKS curl into a ball if they FEEL THREATENED.

A DIVER IN FLORIDA, U.S.A., TOOK A PHOTO OF A **LEMON SHARK** WITH A **TOOTHY GRIN** JUST LIKE **BRUCE**, THE SHARK FROM ***FINDING NEMO.***

Hollywood, here I come!

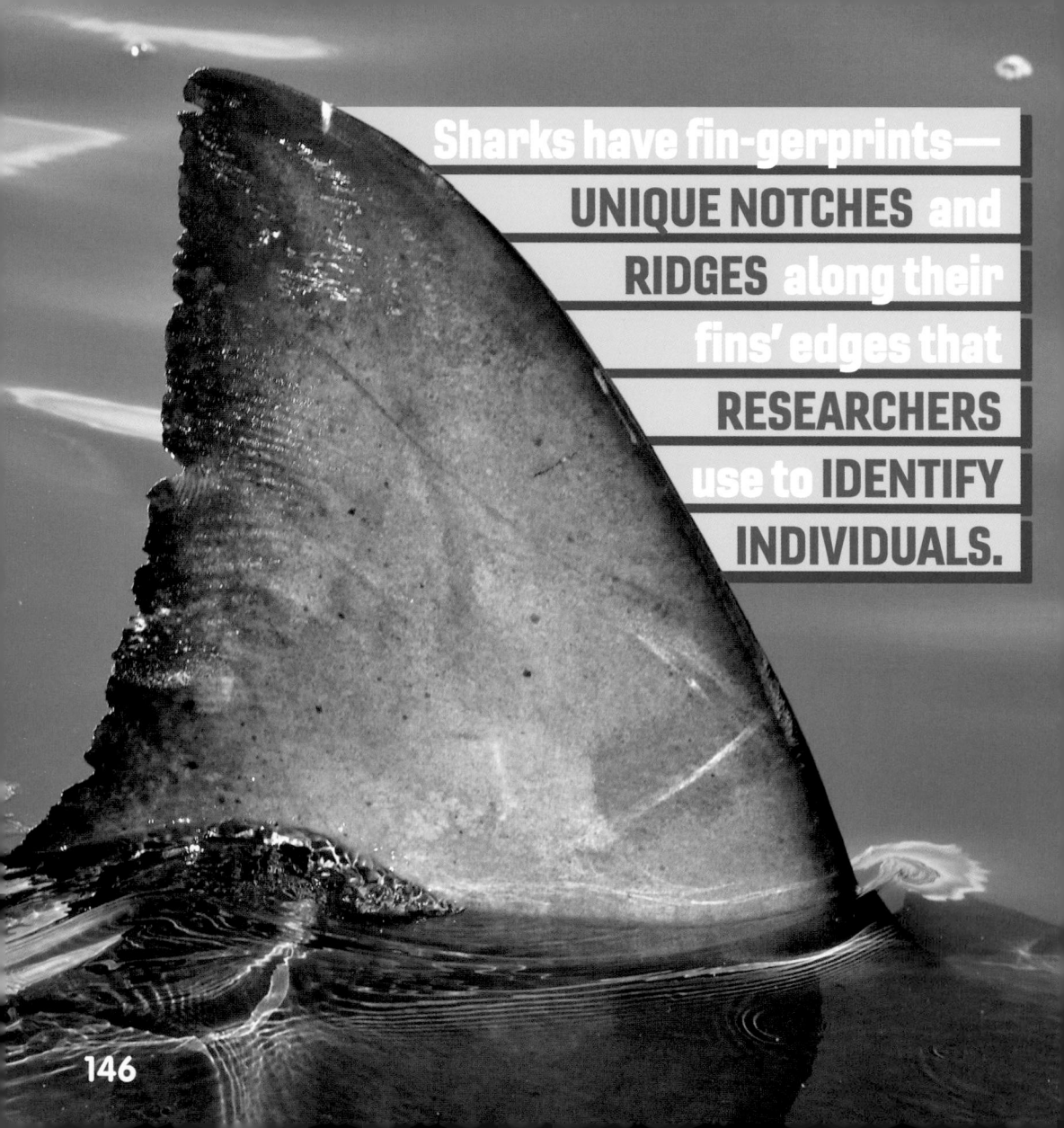

Sharks have fin-gerprints—UNIQUE NOTCHES and RIDGES along their fins' edges that RESEARCHERS use to IDENTIFY INDIVIDUALS.

A SHARK-EYE CAMERA LETS RESEARCHERS **SEE HOW GLOWING SHARKS** APPEAR TO ONE ANOTHER.

The prehistoric **"EAGLE" SHARK'S** fins spanned nearly **six feet** (2 m) from tip to tip.

A researcher taught **captive lemon sharks** to **blink** when **a light flashed**—a skill they mastered **10 times faster** than cats.

Sharks have an **S-shaped heart** and a **U-shaped stomach.**

Venice, Florida, U.S.A., has been called the **"SHARK TOOTH CAPITAL OF THE WORLD"** because so many shark teeth **WASH UP ON ITS SHORES.**

You can rent a **SPECIAL SHOVEL IN VENICE** that lets you sift through sand to **FIND FOSSILS.**

DURING THE 19TH CENTURY, **PACIFIC ISLANDERS**

USED **SWORDS** AND **DAGGERS** WITH **SHARK TEETH** ALONG THE BLADES.

Young tiger sharks have
STRIPES THAT FADE
as they get older.

YOUNG GREAT WHITE SHARKS HAVE **WEAKER BITES** THAN ADULTS BECAUSE THE **CARTILAGE** IN THEIR JAWS HASN'T HARDENED YET.

The nervous shark **HIDES IN THE SEAGRASS** in mangrove forests.

SPYHOPPING

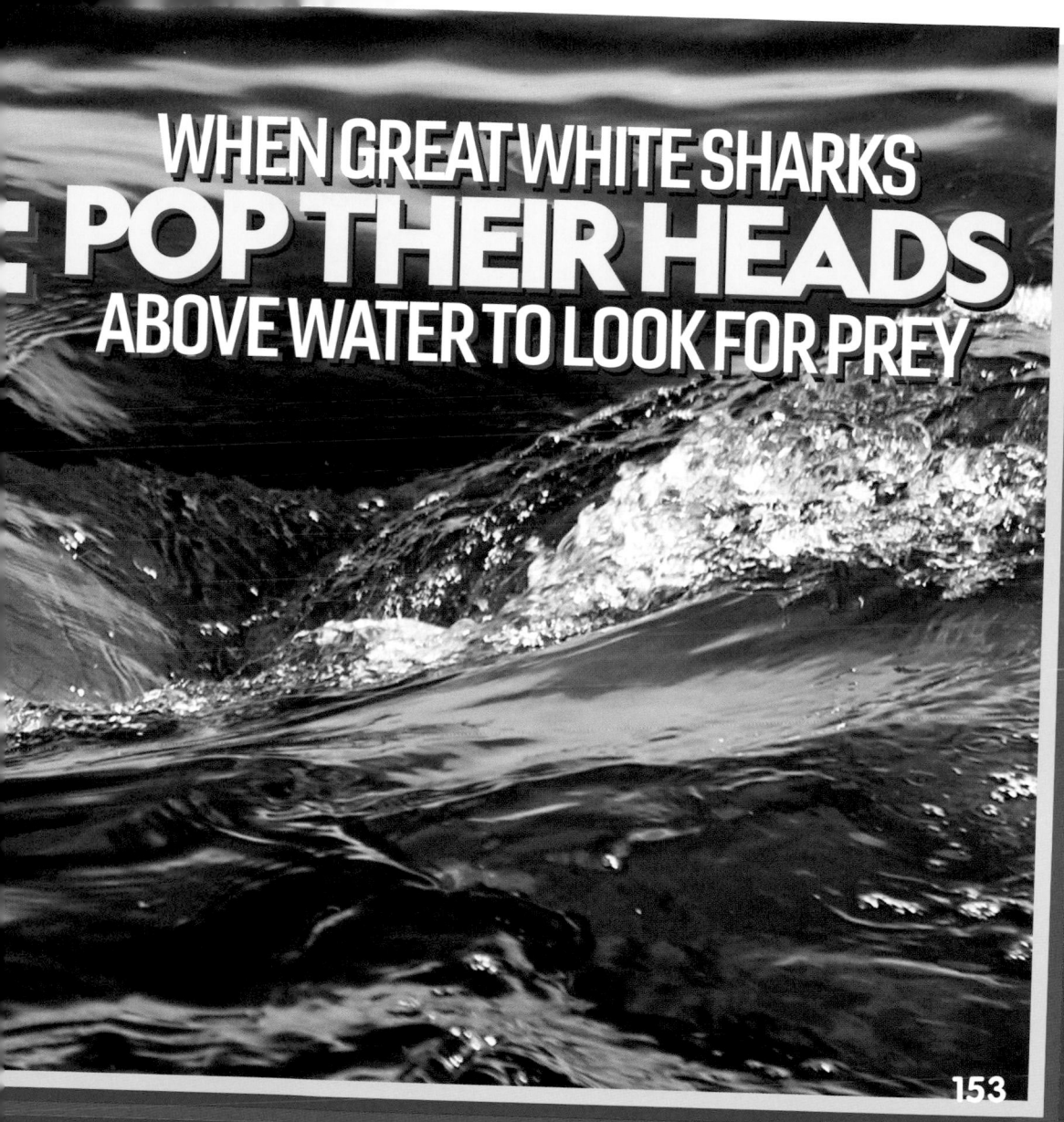
WHEN GREAT WHITE SHARKS
POP THEIR HEADS
ABOVE WATER TO LOOK FOR PREY

Researchers discovered that SHARKS, CAMELS, and LLAMAS
That's weird!
PRODUCE SUBSTANCES in their blood that could be used to TREAT HUMAN DISEASES.

The winghead shark has the **widest head** of all hammerheads—the width is about half as long as the shark's body length.

Pygmy sharks swim up from the ocean floor to **feed at night,** a round-trip distance of nearly **a mile** (1.6 km).

THE "POCKETS" near the pectoral fins of pocket sharks release a **GLOWING SUBSTANCE** they may use **FOR DEFENSE.**

TYLOSAURUS, A MARINE REPTILE CONSIDERED ONE OF THE DEADLIEST HUNTERS

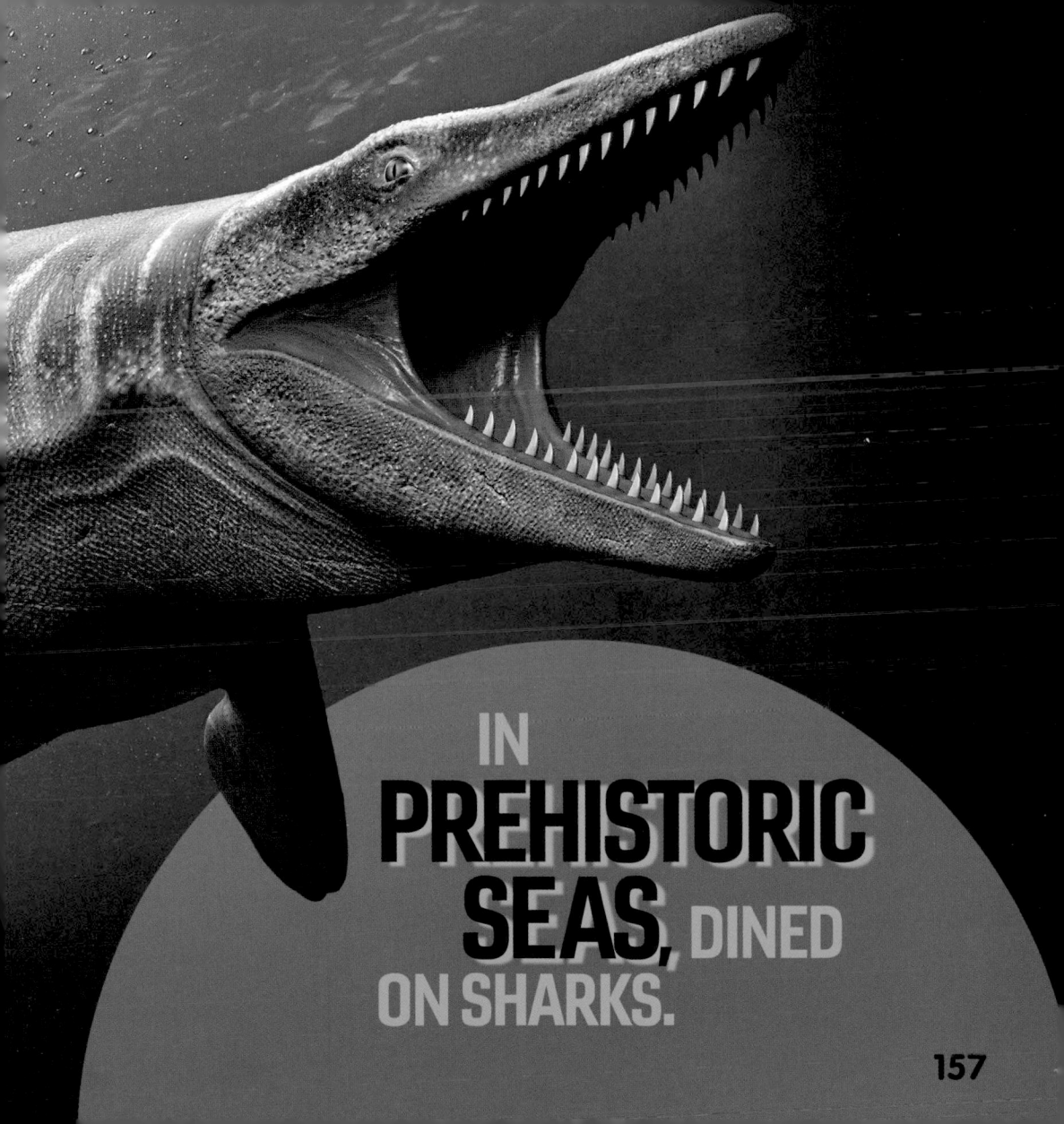

IN PREHISTORIC SEAS, DINED ON SHARKS.

A HOUSE IN OXFORD, ENGLAND, HAS A **26-FOOT** (8-m)**-LONG SHARK** MODEL THAT LOOKS LIKE **IT CRASHED INTO THE ROOF.**

Cookiecutter sharks shed **their lower teeth** and then swallow them.

CLEANER WRASSE FISH SWIM INTO SHARKS' MOUTHS TO EAT UNSWALLOWED FOOD.

Sharks don't have vocal organs,
so they can't make sounds to communicate.

Great white sharks shed their teeth while they're still in the womb.

PUFFADDER SHYSHARKS *curl up*

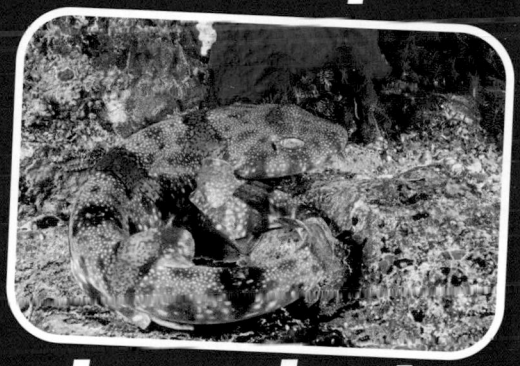

in a circle and use their tails to cover THEIR HEADS.

Spiny dogfish sharks travel and hunt in packs like dogs—that's how they got their name.

In 2005, scientists discovered that a great white shark swam from South Africa to Australia and back again in almost a straight line.

Sharks haven't been able to **survive in Antarctica's cold waters** for some

40

million years.

In 2013, more than

40,000 PEOPLE

on social media followed

LYDIA,

the first great white shark ever recorded **to cross the Atlantic Ocean.**

Thresher sharks use their long tails to SLAP a school of fish,
and then they EAT the ones they've STUNNED.

Baby lemon sharks swim in flooded mangrove "nurseries" that are only knee-high.

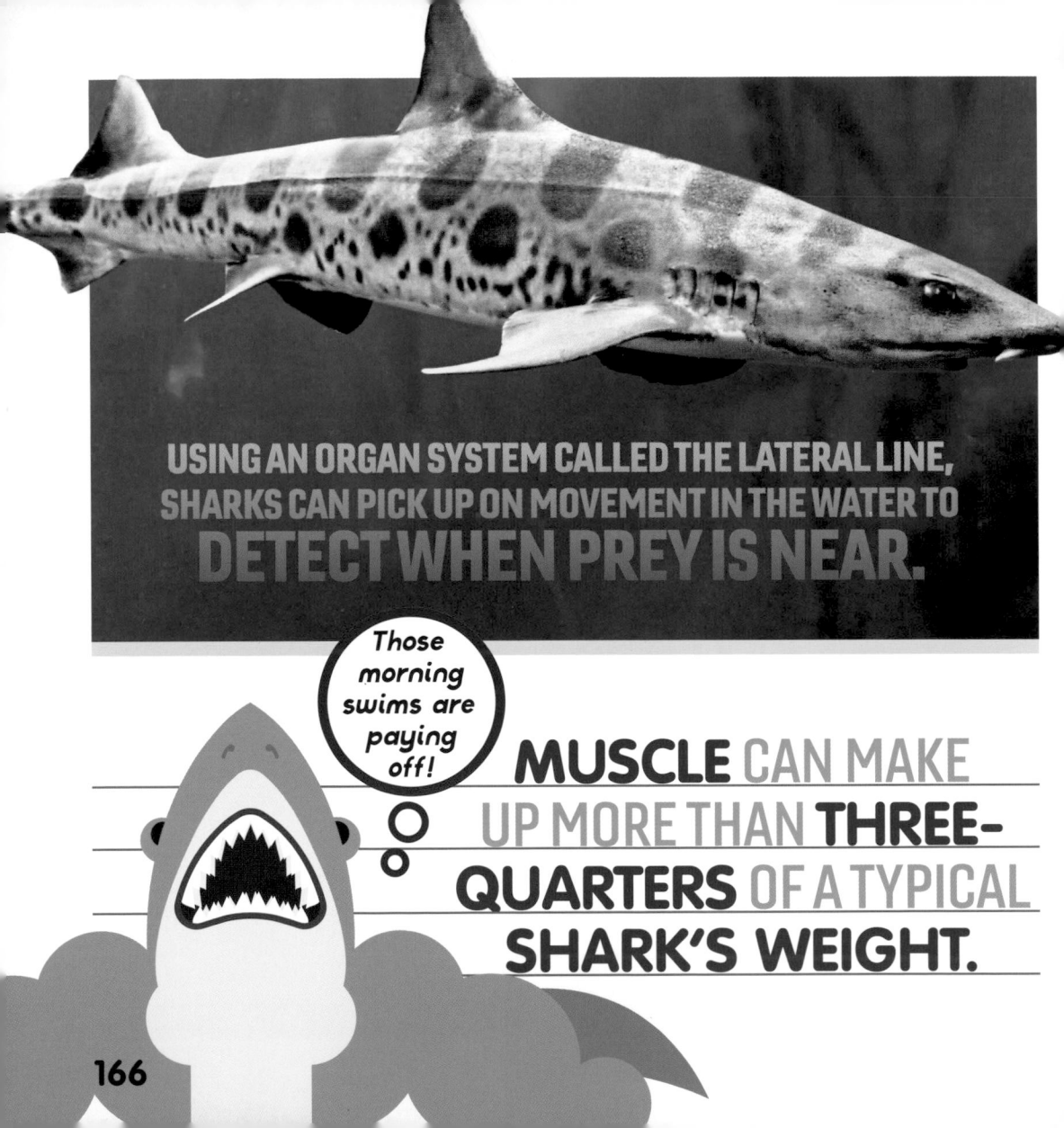
USING AN ORGAN SYSTEM CALLED THE LATERAL LINE, SHARKS CAN PICK UP ON MOVEMENT IN THE WATER TO DETECT WHEN PREY IS NEAR.
Those morning swims are paying off!
MUSCLE CAN MAKE UP MORE THAN THREE-QUARTERS OF A TYPICAL SHARK'S WEIGHT.

Most **shark fossils** are **teeth.**

Shark skin feels like **sandpaper** when rubbed from **tail** to **head.**

FEMALE LEMON SHARKS return to where they were born to **GIVE BIRTH TO THEIR PUPS.**

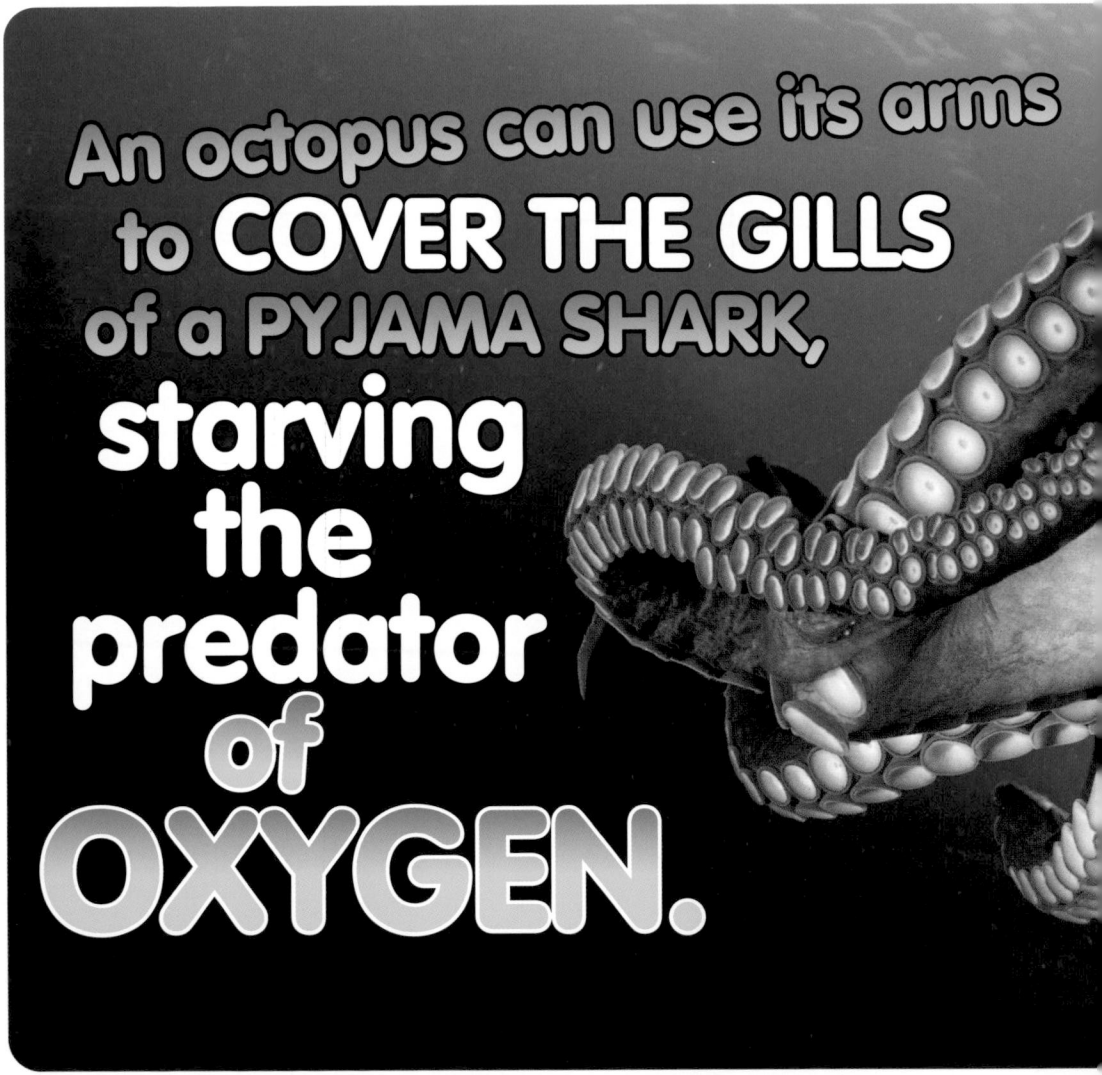
An octopus can use its arms
to COVER THE GILLS
of a PYJAMA SHARK,
starving
the
predator
of
OXYGEN.

Eight arms is the charm!

Sharks can see the color yellow especially well.
Shark researchers jokingly refer to the bright yellow color often found on flotation devices as "YUM-YUM YELLOW."

The draughtsboard shark gulps air, which makes a BARK-LIKE SOUND when released.

Some great white sharks **move their bodies** in an **S shape** when they **poop.**

If your mouth were as comparatively large as a megamouth's, it would be **a foot** (30 cm) **wide.**

In 2008–2009, the **San Jose Sharks** scored **52 points** in their first 30 games—the best start to a season by a **professional hockey team.**

Some sharks
can survive
for several hours
out of water.
Swell sharks
gulp water and
balloon
to twice their
normal size
to protect
themselves.

MORE THAN THREE-QUARTERS OF
SHARK SPECIES WILL
RARELY SEE A HUMAN
OR ARE UNABLE TO
EAT HUMANS.

The massive "Planet Ocean" mural in Long Beach, California, U.S.A., features life-size sharks.

It took 7,000 gallons (26,500 L) of paint to create the 1,280-foot (390-m)-long mural.

Scientists got a great white shark to **swallow a tracking device** by **wrapping it in seal fat,** which they called

A BLUBBER BURRITO.

THE WATERS OF
THE GALÁPAGOS ISLANDS
ARE HOME TO
34
SPECIES
OF
SHARK.

Olympic swimmers have worn swimsuits modeled on shark skin.
Hello, little friends!
A whale shark can weigh about as

Swimmers at an underwater park in Palm Beach County, Florida, U.S.A., can snorkel around three **1,500-pound** (680-kg) hammerhead statues.

much as five large African elephants.

At the
ALBUQUERQUE
INTERNATIONAL
BALLOON
FIESTA in New
Mexico, U.S.A.,
a shark-
shaped hot-
air balloon
took to the
SKIES.

Most female sharks
lose their appetite before giving birth, which prevents them from
eating their own pups.

THE INSIDE OF
A MEGAMOUTH
SHARK'S
MOUTH
GLOWS TO
ATTRACT
PREY.

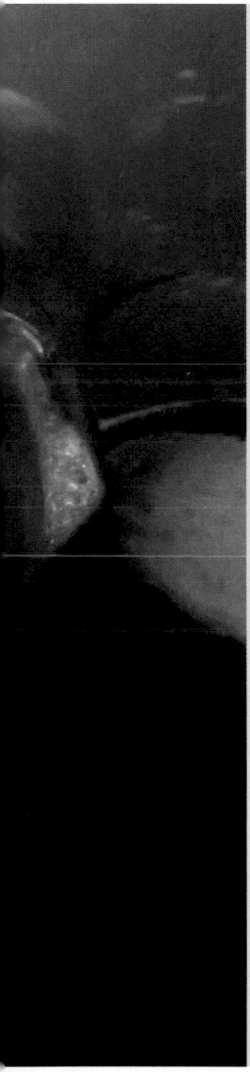

SHARKS IN AQUARIUMS ARE KNOWN TO

SPIT OUT

THEIR VITAMINS.

Each tooth in the ANCIENT CLADODONT SHARK'S mouth had A SINGLE SPIKE

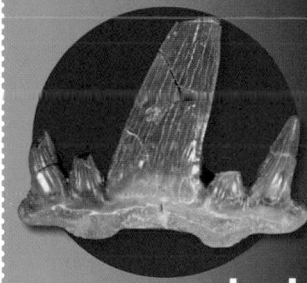

surrounded by smaller SPIKES.

Sharks range in
size from the
length of a pencil
to a
SCHOOL BUS.
STOP

VISITORS WHO STAND BY A **GIANT SHARK MURAL** IN ST. PETERSBURG, FLORIDA, U.S.A., LOOK LIKE THEY ARE ABOUT TO GET **CHOMPED.**

Megalodon's
head
was
about
as long
as an
SUV.

Whale shark skin—the thickest of any animal's—is about as thick as a stack of **58** quarters.

An ancient Hawaiian legend tells of a kind shark that **left food** on the beach every day for an elderly couple to **eat.**

More than **100 SPECIES OF SHARK** swim off the coast of **SOUTH AFRICA.**

Swordfish sometimes kill sharks with their

LONG, POINTED BILLS.

Bull sharks have traveled up the Mississippi River as far north as St. Louis, Missouri, U.S.A.

Spinner sharks leap out of the water and spin like a football several times before splashing back into the ocean.
ANGEL SHARKS SOMETIMES sit camouflaged on the seafloor for days, STRIKING WHEN PREY SWIMS BY.
Hush! I'm hiding.

A COMPANY WORKING TO CAPTURE ENERGY FROM OCEAN TIDES MODELED ITS MACHINES AFTER THE MOVEMENT OF SHARK FINS.

THE MAKO ROLLER COASTER AT SEAWORLD IN ORLANDO, FLORIDA, U.S.A., REACHES SPEEDS FASTER THAN A CAR ON A HIGHWAY.

Greenland sharks have **compounds in their bodies** that act like a **natural antifreeze,** allowing them to swim in the **Arctic's cold waters.**

The molecules that cause some sharks to **GLOW GREEN** may also help protect them from diseases.

During the late Cretaceous, part of what is today Alabama, U.S.A., was underwater and a hotbed for *SHARKS.*

Horn sharks use their **pelvic fins** to scoot along the ocean floor.

PEOPLE ARE A MUCH **BIGGER DANGER** TO SHARKS **THAN** SHARKS ARE TO PEOPLE.

Sharks have

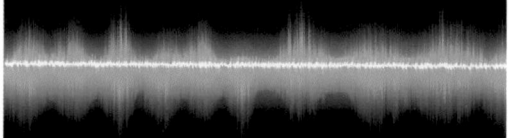

INTERNAL EARS.

Cat sharks not only **glow**—they glow in **specific patterns.**

Artist Damien Hirst created a work that displayed a *PRESERVED DEAD TIGER SHARK* in a **GLASS CASE.**

Shark poop is **YELLOW-GREEN.**

THRESHER SHARKS CAN WHIP THEIR TAILS AT PREY AS FAST AS **80 MILES AN HOUR** (129 km/h).

A whale shark's heart weighs more than three basketballs.

THE CONSTELLATION **BAIDAM,** MADE UP OF THE STARS IN THE BIG DIPPER, IS **SHAPED LIKE A SHARK.**

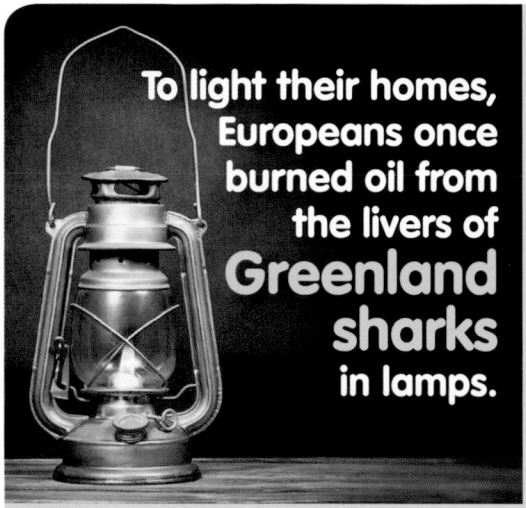

To light their homes, Europeans once burned oil from the livers of **Greenland sharks** in lamps.

HORN SHARKS INJECT VENOM INTO PREDATORS BY USING TWO SHORT HORNS IN FRONT OF THEIR DORSAL FINS.

Blue sharks are named for the **unique color** of their **skin.**

An ancient shark nicknamed
the "GODZILLA"
SHARK had 12 ROWS
OF SHARP TEETH.

In the movie **Deep Blue Sea,** filmmakers used equipment found in **airplanes** to create the **animatronic mako shark.**

SCIENTISTS IN NOVA SCOTIA, CANADA, TAGGED A **17-FOOT (5.2-m)-LONG, 3,541-POUND (1,606-kg)** GREAT WHITE SHARK THEY CALL **"QUEEN OF THE OCEAN."**

Golfers putt alongside about **12 BULL SHARKS** that live in a lake on a Queensland, Australia, golf course.

Archaeologists discovered the **3,000-year-old skeletal** remains of a man attacked **by a shark in Japan.**

Researchers **MEASURE** extinct sharks' fossilized **TEETH** to **ESTIMATE** the **ANIMALS' SIZE.**

Boldface indicates illustrations.

A

Algae 77
Alligators 88, **88**
Angel sharks 93, **93,** 190, **190**
Animatronic shark 198, **198**
Antarctica 163, **163**
Aquariums 183
Art
  murals 38, **38,** 176, **176,** 185, **185**
  preserved tiger shark 195
  shark cake 115, **115**
  shark head 138, **138**
  from trash 112–113, **112–113**
  underwater statues 179, **179**
Attacks on humans 83, 129, 199

B

Babies *see* Pups
"Baby Shark" video 50, **50**
Baidam (constellation) 195
Balance 64
Barnacles 77
Baseball 46, **46,** 50
Basking sharks
  common name 64
  pups 57
  snout 89, **89**
  stomach size 73
  water filtered by **68–69,** 69
Benchley, Peter 31
Bioluminescence *see* Glowing sharks
Blinking 15, 148, **148**
Blood detection 91
Blood substances 154
Blubber burrito 176
Blue sharks 104, **104,** 136, **136,** 196, **196**
Bonnethead sharks **16–17,** 17, 30, **30,** 88, **88**
Brain 77
Breathing 67
Buildings **54–55,** 55, 103, **103,** 158, **158**
Bull sharks
  as aquarium rarity 87
  in golf course lake 199, **199**
  headbutting 5, **5**
  Mississippi River 189, **189**
  and remoras 92, **92**
  size 27

C

Cakes 115, **115**
Camels 154, **154**
Camouflage 131, **131,** 190, **190**
Cape fur seals 104, **104**
Car, named for shark 119, **119**
Caribbean reef sharks 84, **84–85**
Cartilage 139, 151
Cat sharks
  communication **62–63,** 63
  egg cases 91, **91**
  eyes 127, **127**
  glowing in patterns 194, **194**
  size 123, **123**
Cladodont sharks 183, **183**
Cleaner wrasse fish 159, **159**
Color
  blue sharks 196, **196**
  changing 131, **131**
  fossilized teeth 139
  goblin sharks 15, **15**
  great white sharks 131, **131**
  horn sharks' spines 67
  lemon sharks 51, **51**
  shark poop 195
  teeth stained by sea urchins 64
Color vision 31, 170
Communication 63, 160
Cookiecutter sharks 12, 18, **18,** 158
Crocodile poop 70, **70**
Crocodile sharks 72

D

Deep Blue Sea (movie) 198, **198**
Dermal denticles 5, **5**
Digestion 101
Dinosaurs, eaten by sharks 106
Dorsal fins 83, **83,** 140, **140–141**

Draughtsboard sharks 171, **171**

E

"Eagle" shark 147
Ears 64, 194
Edestus 10, **10**
Egg cases 4, **4,** 11, **11,** 91, **91**; *see also* Unborn sharks
Electrical currents 40
Elephant sharks *see* Basking sharks
Elephants 178–179, **178–179**
Etmopterus benchleyi 31
Extinct sharks *see* Prehistoric sharks
Extinctions, shark survival 39
Eyelids 109, **109**
Eyes
  age estimates 47
  blinking 15
  cat sharks 127, **127**
  color vision 31
  covered by teeth 109, **109**
  hammerhead sharks 13, **13**
  parasites 22
  shining in dark 173, **173**
  size 122, **122**
Eyesight 31, 127, 170

F

Falcatus **132–133,** 133
Finding Dory (movie) 90, **90**
Finding Nemo (movie) 144
Fins
  as energy model 191
  fin-gerprints 146, **146**
  scooting along ocean floor 193
  shape 60, **60–61,** 83, **83, 132–133,** 133
  span 147
  with spines 140, **140–141**
Fossilized poop 37, **37,** 70, **70**
Fossilized scales 41, **41**
Fossilized teeth *see* Teeth
Freshwater sharks 18, **18**
Friendships 20
Frilled sharks 51, 83, **100–101,** 101, 139, **139**

G

Galápagos fur seals 78, **78**
Galápagos Islands 177, **177**
Galápagos sharks 45, 76, **76**
Gills 67
"Ginsu" shark **110–111,** 111
Glowing sharks
  attracting prey 182, **182–183**
  defense 155
  disease protection 193
  largest 19, **19**
  patterns 194, **194**
  "shark-eye camera" 147
  sneaking up on prey 110, **110–111**
Goblin sharks 15, **15,** 52, **52–53**
"Godzilla" shark 197, **197**
Golf course 199, **199**
Goliath groupers 79, **79**
Gray reef sharks 20
Great white sharks
  in art 112–113, **112–113**
  attacking prey 82, **82**
  attacks on humans 129
  bite force 151
  blood detection 91
  camouflage 131, **131**
  eating style 41
  growth rate **124–125,** 125
  Jaws (movie) 74–75, **74–75**
  leaping 82, **82**
  liver 8–9, **9**
  migration 67, 162, **162,** 163, **163**
  poop 142, 172, **172**
  predators 8, **8–9,** 36, **36–37**
  "queen of the ocean" 199
  shedding teeth before birth 161
  size 70, **70**
  size of newborn 118, **118**
  on social media 163, **163**
  spyhopping 152–153, **152–153**
  tracking devices 176
Greenland sharks
  eating land animals 19
  eye parasites 22
  as food for humans 124–125

lifespan 47
livers 196
natural antifreeze 193
reproduction 87, **87**
swimming speed 20, **20**

H

Hákarl ("rotten shark") 124–125
Hammerhead sharks
eyes 13, **13**
head 21, **21,** 120, **120,** 155, **155**
hearing 5
living inside volcanoes 119
nostrils 13, **13**
swimming style 120, **120**
underwater statues 179, **179**
winghead sharks 155, **155**
Hammerheads (baseball team) 46, **46**
Heart 149, 195
Hirst, Damien 195
Hockey 173, **173**
Horn sharks 64, 67, 128, **128,** 193, 196
Hot-air balloons 180, **180**
Humans
as danger to sharks 194
disease treatments 154
eating fermented shark 124–125
fish stolen by sharks 136, **136**
as predators 36
rarity of shark encounters 175
shark attacks on 83, 129, 199
shark teeth in swords and daggers 149, **149**
snorkeling 179, **179**

I

Iguanas **44–45,** 45
Indigenous people 79
Inflatable shark **54–55,** 55
Innkeeper worms 29
Intestines 19, **19**

J

Jaws
crocodile sharks 72
Edestus 10, **10**
extendable 18
great white sharks 151
not attached to skull 71, **71**
viper dogfish 18
see also Teeth
Jaws (Benchley novel) 31
Jaws (movie) 74–75, **74–75,** 102, 121, **121,** 141

K

Kavachi 119
Kitefin sharks (Sharkcano) 19, **19**

L

Lateral line 166, **166**
Legends 187
Lemon sharks
alligator attacks on 88, **88**
birth location 167
blinking 148, **148**
detecting tuna juice 151
mangrove "nurseries" 165
personalities 59, **59**
skin color 51, **51**
smiling 144, **144–145**
Leopard sharks 29, **29**
Lifespan 47
Liver 8–9, 196
Llamas 154, **154**

M

Mackerel sharks 31, **31**
Mako Roller Coaster 192, **192**
Mako sharks 87, 119, **119,** 129, **129,** 198, **198**
Maps 32, 34–35, 188
Marine iguanas **44–45,** 45
Mascots 46, **46**
Mechanical sharks 121, **121**
Megalodon
amount eaten by 56–57
head size 186, **186**
museum model 116, **116–117**
size 70, **70,** 86, **86**
teeth 86

Megalodon (monster truck) 108, **108**
Megamouth sharks 49, **49,** 173, 182, **182–183**
Mermaid purses *see* Egg cases
Meru Peak, India 103, **103**
Middle Ages 97
Migration
  great white sharks 67, 162, **162,** 163, **163**
  megamouth sharks 49, **49**
  shortfin mako sharks 62
  vertical 155
Mississippi River 189, **189**
Monster trucks 108, **108**
Movement detection 81
Murals 38, **38,** 176, **176,** 185, **185**
Muscle 166

N

Navigation 30
Nervous sharks 151
Ninja lanternshark 110–111, **110–111**
Nostrils 13, **13**; *see also* Snout
Nurse sharks 67, 88, **88,** 95, **95**

O

Oceanic whitetip sharks 66, **66,** 73
Octopuses 26, 168, **168–169**
Olympics 178, **178**
Orcas 8, **8–9,** 36, **36–37**
Orthacanthus 98, **98–99**

P

Pacific Islanders 149
Pacific Ocean sanctuaries 32
Parasites 22
Parra, Gerardo 50
Pelvic fins 193
Plesiosaurs 135
Pocket sharks 155
Poop and pooping
  color 195
  eaten by fish 142
  fossilized poop 37, **37,** 70, **70**
  great white sharks 142, 172, **172**
  spiral-shaped 105
  tapeworm eggs in 37, **37**
Porbeagles 31, **31**
Port Jackson sharks 11, **11**
Prehistoric sharks
  Alabama, U.S.A. 193
  attack on plesiosaur 135
  "eagle" shark's fin span 147
  Edestus 10, **10**
  Falcatus **132–133,** 133
  "ginsu" shark **110–111,** 111
  "Godzilla" shark 197, **197**
  megalodon 56–57, 70, **70,** 86, **86,** 116, **116–117,** 186, **186**
  Orthacanthus 98, **98–99**
  predators 156–157, **156–157**
  Ptychodus teeth 137, **137**
  size estimates 199
  Squalicorax 106, **106**
  Stethacanthus 60, **60–61**
  Xenacanthus 58, **58**
Pterosaurs 106
Ptychodus 137, **137**
Puffadder shysharks 161, **161**
Pups
  birth location 167
  eaten by parents 98, 181
  eating each other 41
  hammerhead sharks 120, **120**
  mangrove "nurseries" 165
  markings 94, **94**
  number of 29
  personalities 59, **59**
  size 57, 118, **118**
Purple sea urchins 67, **67**
Pygmy ribbontail cat sharks 123, **123**
Pygmy sharks 155
Pyjama sharks 14, **14,** 76, 143, **143,** 168

R

Red sea urchins 64, **64**
Remora fish 42–43, **42–43,** 92, **92**
Robots 63, **63**
Roller coasters 192, **192**
Rubber shark collection 62

S

Salmon sharks 129
San Jose Sharks 173, **173**
Sanctuaries 32
Sand sharks 33, **33**
Sand tiger sharks 41, 105, **105**
Sawfish 98
Saw sharks 22, **22,** 88, **88–89**
Scales 29, 41, **41**
Scalloped hammerheads 119
Sea urchins 64, **64,** 67, **67**
Seals 56, **56,** 104, **104**
SeaWorld, Orlando, Florida, U.S.A. 192, **192**
Senses
  blood detection 91
  color vision 31, 170
  detecting tuna juice 151
  electrical currents 40
  eyesight in low light 127, **127**
  lateral line 166, **166**
  movement detection 81
  smell 77
Sevengill sharks 91, **91**
Shark Awareness Day 51
Shark cams 147, **147**
Shark repellent 126
Shark sanctuaries 32
Sharkcano 119
Shark's Fin (granite wall) 103, **103**
Ships 12, **12,** 77, 80, **80–81**
Shortfin mako sharks **52–53,** 53, 62, 65, **65,** 191
Silky sharks 119
Size
  basking shark pups 57
  bull sharks 27
  great white shark 70, **70**
  megalodon 70, **70,** 86, **86,** 186, **186**
  pygmy ribbontail cat sharks 123, **123**
  range 184, **184**
  whale sharks 178–179, **178–179,** 195
Skin
  dermal denticles 5, **5**
  expanding **100–101,** 101
  feeling like sandpaper 167
  resistance to barnacles and algae 77
  scales 29, 41, **41**
  swimsuits modeled on 178, **178**
  thickness 19, 187, **187**
  yoga mat modeled on 137
  see also Color
Smell, sense of 77
Snaggletooth shark 134, **134**
Snout 13, **13,** 22, **22,** 40, 89, **89**
Social media 163, **163**
Songbirds 33, **33**
Speed 20, **20,** 53, 65, **65,** 129, **129**
Spinner sharks 190, **190**
Spiny dogfish sharks 140, **140–141,** 162, **162**
Spyhopping 152–153, **152–153**
Squalicorax 106, **106**
Stethacanthus 60, **60–61**
Stingrays 21
Stomach
  acids 105
  contents 15, **15**
  digestion 101
  pushed out of mouth and rinsed off 99, **99**
  shape 149
  size 73
Submarines 12, **12,** 80, **80–81**
Swell sharks 174, **174**
Swimming
  inability to swim backward 92
  in loops 114, **114**
  speed 20, **20,** 65, **65,** 129, **129**
  tail swish 81
  tilted to one side 120, **120**
Swimsuits modeled on shark skin 178, **178**
Swordfish **188–189,** 189

T

Tails 80, 81, 164–165, **164–165,** 195
Tapeworm eggs 37
Teeth
  color of fossilized teeth 139

covering eyes 109, **109**
diving for fossilized teeth 142
fluoride covering 87
fossilization time 107, **107**
as Georgia state fossil 79
"Godzilla" shark 197, **197**
megalodon 86
Middle Ages beliefs 23, 97
as most common shark fossil 167, **167**
new sets 32, **32**
number in a lifetime 96
sand tiger sharks 105, **105**
saw sharks 88, **88–89**
serrated 28
sevengill sharks 91, **91**
shaped like garbage can lids 137, **137**
shark cake 115, **115**
"shark tooth capital of the world" 149
shed by unborn sharks 161
in size estimates 199
snaggletooth shark 134, **134**
spikes 183, **183**
stained by sea urchins 64
swallowing shed teeth 158
tiger sharks 28, 87
trident-shaped 51
use by humans 79, **79,** 149, **149**
whale sharks 109, **109**
Thresher sharks 164–165, **164–165,** 195
Tiger sharks
in art 195
markings 150, **150**
preying on songbirds 33
stomach contents 15, **15**
swimming in loops 114, **114**
teeth 28, 87
Tracking devices 176
Trancelike state 48
Trash, art from 112–113, **112–113**
Tuna 66, 151
Turtles **28**
Tylosaurus 156–157, **156–157**

U

Unborn sharks 41, 61, **61,** 161; *see also* Egg cases
Underwater vehicles 12, **12,** 80, **80–81**
United States Navy 77, 126

V

Viper dogfish 18
Vision 31, 127, 170
Vitamins, spit out by sharks 183
Volcanoes, underwater 119

W

Walking sharks 12, **12**
Washington Nationals 50
WasteShark 63, **63**
Waterslides 72, **72**
Whale sharks
Finding Dory (movie) 90, **90**
heart weight 195
as largest fish 48, **48**
number of pups 29
size of newborn 118
skin thickness 187, **187**
spot pattern 6–7, **6–7,** 97, **97**
teeth covering eyes 109, **109**
weight compared to elephants 178–179, **178–179**
"White Shark Café" 67
Whitetip reef sharks 26, **26,** 79, **79**
Winghead sharks 155, **155**
Wobbegong sharks 24–25, **24–25**

X

Xenacanthus 58, **58**

Z

Zebra sharks 94, **94**

Copyright © 2023 National Geographic Partners, LLC. All rights reserved. Reproduction of the whole or any part of the contents without written permission from the publisher is prohibited.

NATIONAL GEOGRAPHIC and Yellow Border Design are trademarks of the National Geographic Society, used under license.

Since 1888, the National Geographic Society has funded more than 14,000 research, conservation, education, and storytelling projects around the world. National Geographic Partners distributes a portion of the funds it receives from your purchase to National Geographic Society to support programs including the conservation of animals and their habitats. To learn more, visit natgeo.com/info.

For more information, visit nationalgeographic.com, call 1-877-873-6846, or write to the following address:

National Geographic Partners, LLC
1145 17th Street NW
Washington, DC 20036-4688 U.S.A.

For librarians and teachers: nationalgeographic.com/books/librarians-and-educators

More for kids from National Geographic: natgeokids.com

National Geographic Kids magazine inspires children to explore their world with fun yet educational articles on animals, science, nature, and more. Using fresh storytelling and amazing photography, *Nat Geo Kids* shows kids ages 6 to 14 the fascinating truth about the world—and why they should care.
natgeo.com/subscribe

For rights or permissions inquiries, please contact National Geographic Books Subsidiary Rights: bookrights@natgeo.com

The publisher would like to thank the fin-tastic book team: Michelle Harris and Julie Beer, writers; Grace Hill and Kathryn Williams, editors; Julide Dengel, designer; Sarah Mock, photo editor; Robin Palmer, researcher; Molly Reid, production editor; and Gus Tello, designer.

Trade paperback ISBN: 978-1-4263-7240-7
Reinforced library binding ISBN: 978-1-4263-7241-4

Printed in China
22/PPS/1

PHOTO CREDITS

AL = Alamy Stock Photo; AS = Adobe Stock; GI = Getty Images; SS = Shutterstock

Cover (UP CTR), Sean/AS; (UP RT), Doug Perrine/Nature Picture Library; (LO RT), Andy Murch/Image Quest Marine; (LO LE), EXTREME-PHOTOGRAPHER/GI; (CTR LE), Wildestanimal/AL; Spine, Wildestanimal/AL; Back Cover, bullet_chained/AS; 1 (BACKGROUND), Romolo Tavani/AS; 2-3 (BACKGROUND), Romolo Tavani/AS; 2, wildestanimal/SS; 3, Sergey Uryadnikov/Dreamstime; 4 (BACKGROUND), bayqpatterns/SS; 4 (UP LE), hanahusain/SS; 4 (dog), Kimberly Reinick/AS; 4 (hat), Aleksangel/SS; 4 (RT), Andrea Izzotti/AS; 5 (LE), Fiona Ayerst/SS; 5 (LO RT), Will Schubert/Blue Planet Archive; 6-7, Krzysztof Odziomek/Dreamstime; 6-7 (fingerprints), Andrey Kuzmin/AS; 8, Mike Price/SS; 8-9 (CTR), bekirevren/AS; 9, wildestanimal/AS; 10, Franco Tempesta; 11 (LE), Doug Perrine/Blue Planet Archive; 11 (RT), HollyHarry/AS; 12 (UP), Ethan Daniels/Blue Planet Archive; 12 (LO), muchmania/AS; 13, frantisekhojdysz/SS; 14, wildestanimal/GI; 15 (UP), Makoto Hirose/e-Photo/Blue Planet Archive; 15 (LO LE), toricheks/AS; 15 (LO RT), Dmitry Kalinovsky/SS; 16-17, Shane Gross/Nature Picture Library; 18 (UP), Jeff Milisen/Blue Planet Archive; 18 (LO), wildestanimal/AS; 19 (CTR LE), Jerome Mallefet; 19 (LO RT), Eric Isselée/AS; 19 (LO CTR), Samantha Leigh, PhD; 20 (UP), dottedyeti/AS; 20 (LO), oxyggen/AS; 21, wildestanimal/AS; 22 (UP), Sabine/AS; 22 (LO), MicroOne/SS; 23, Veronika Surovtseva/SS; 24-25, the Ocean Agency/AS; 26, David P. Fleetham/Blue Planet Archive; 26 (CTR LE), Happypictures/AS; 27, Alhovik/Dreamstime; 28, Happy monkey/AS; 29 (LE), Jelger Herder/Buiten-Beeld/AL; 29 (BACKGROUND), gepard/AS; 29 (RT), natrot/AS; 30 (LE), maryartist/SS; 30 (RT), Irina K./AS; 31 (UP LE), klyaksun/AS; 31 (shark), Yves Lefèvre/Biosphoto; 31 (LO RT), Zebra Finch/AS; 31 (LO LE), 2DAssets/SS; 32 (UP), NG Maps; 32 (LO), jonnysek/AS; 33 (UP), Michael Woodruff/SS; 34-35 (BACKGROUND), Kundra/AS; 34-35 (CTR), NG Maps; 34 (UP), Eric Isselée/AS; 34 (LO), zimagine/AS; 35 (UP), AvetPhotos/SS; 35 (LO), Rich Carey/SS; 36-37, wildestanimal/AS; 37 (LO LE), timtimphoto/AS; 37 (RT), Breck P. Kent/SS; 38, Mr. Yoshi; 39, Esteban De Armas/SS; 40, Andy Murch/Image Quest Marine; 41 (UP), yekaterinalim/AS; 41 (LO), Erin Dillon & Jorge Ceballos; 42, Mauricio Handler/GI; 43, VisionDiveAS; 46 (ball), Willard/GI; 44-45, Tomas Kotouc/SS; 46 (LO), Greg Lovett/Palm Beach Post/ZUMAPRESS; 47, Lana/AS; 48 (UP), Adam/AS; 48 (LO RT), Annity Art/SS; 48 (LO LE), GalapagosPhoto/SS; 49, Bruce Rasner/Blue Planet Archive; 50 (BACKGROUND), augustos/SS; 50 (CTR), Olga Lebedeva/SS; 50 (shark), Magic world of design/SS; 51 (UP), Alex Mustard/Nature Picture Library; 51 (LO RT), Design Studio RM/AS; 51 (calendar), Jane Kelly/AS; 51 (icon), Eriska melody/AS; 52 (UP), Kelvin Aitken/VWPics/AL; 52 (LO), wildestanimal/SS; 54-55, TRIPPLAAR KRISTOFFER/SIPA/Newscom; 56 (UP), Westend61/GI; 57 (UP), estudio Maia/SS; 56-57 (LO), Joe Belanger/SS; 58, Mauricio Alvarez Abel; 59, Shane Gross/Nature Picture Library; 59 (masks), sudowoodo/AS; 60, Franco Tempesta; 61, Papilio/AL; 62 (UP), Red Monkey/AS; 63 (UP), RanMarine; 62-63 (LO), David Gruber; 64 (UP), cherylvb/AS; 64 (LO), lukaspuchrik/AS; 65, Andy Murch/Image Quest Marine; 66 (BACKGROUND), whitcomberd/AS; 66, Ken Kiefer 2/GI; 67 (RT), cherylvb/AS; 67 (LE), Andrey_Kuzmin/SS; 68-69, Grant M Henderson/SS; 70 (UP), Dr. Stepnen Goafrey/Calvert Marine Museum; 70 (LO LE), Tom/AS; 70 (LO RT), mark/AS; 71, Klaus Jost/Blue Planet Archive; 72 (LE), Atlantis Paradise Island/Mega/Newscom; 72 (CTR), Jochen Tack/AL; 73 (LE), primopiano/SS; 73 (RT), Bambang TJ/SS; 74-75 (ALL), Universal Pictures/Photofest; 76 (UP), Masa Ushioda/Blue Planet Archive; 76 (LO LE), Pavel Talashov/SS; 77 (UP), Alessandro De Maddalena/GI; 77 (LO), Afanasia/AS; 78, Noel/AS; 78 (INSET), Fernando Astasio Avila/SS; 79 (UP), Tsado/AS; 79 (LO RT), endstern/AS; 79 (LO LE), Doug Perrine/Nature Picture Library; 80, Kovalenko I/AS; 81, Annity Art/SS; 82, Sergey Uryadnikov/SS; 83 (UP LE), Olga_i/SS; 83 (LO LE), preto_perola/AS; 83 (RT), fotoyou/AS; 84-85, Michael Bogner/AS; 86 (UP), bergamont/SS; 86 (LO), ratpack223/AS; 86 (diver), ashva73/AS; 87 (UP), Doug Perrine/Blue Planet Archive; 87 (LO RT), cookiechoo/AS; 87 (LO LE), Jessica/AS; 88-89 (UP), Makoto Kubo/e-Photo/Blue Planet Archive; 88 (LO), Eric Isselee/SS; 89 (LO), Alex Mustard/Nature Picture Library; 90, Walt Disney Studios Motion Pictures/Photofest; 91 (LE), Doug Perrine/Blue Planet Archive; 91 (UP RT), percom/SS; 91 (LO RT), SBS Eclectic Images/AL; 92 (UP), Fiona Ayerst/SS; 92 (LO), olando/AS; 93, Andy Murch/Blue Planet Archive; 94 (UP), Rich Carey/SS; 94 (bones), Titima Ongkantong/SS; 94 (LO), nerthuz/AS; 95, Artur/AS; 95 (pacifier), Farah Sadikhova/SS; 97 (LE), Brandelet/SS; 97 (RT), topvectors/AS; 98-99 (UP), MR1805/GI; 98 (LO), JIANG HONGYAN/SS; 99 (LO LE), focus_bell/AS; 99 (LO RT), liloocola/AS; 100-101, Kelvin Aitken/V&W/Image Quest Marine; 102, Dendy Harya/SS; 103 (LE), Zoonar/Galyna Andrushko/AL; 103 (RT), (Joaquín Espinoza); 104, wildestanimal/SS; 105 (UP), Daniel Hernanz Ramos/GI; 105 (LO RT), Soulartist/SS; 105 (LO LE), Supza/SS; 106, Mark Witton; 107, Mark_Kostich/SS; 108, Paulo Lopes/Zuma Wire; 109, Krzysztof Odziomek/Dreamstime; 110 (UP), Millard H. Sharp/Science Source; 110 (LO), Vicky Vasquez; 112-113, Washed Ashore; 112-113 (trash cans), antto/AS; 114, yoshinori/AS; 115 (BACKGROUND), paketesama/AS; 115 (LE), Q77photo/AS; 115 (RT), Cindy Ord/GI; 116-117, John Whitaker; 118 (UP), Nerthuz/SS; 118 (CTR), Nomadsoul1/Dreamstime; 118 (LO), Evikka/SS; 119 (UP), Uli Jooss/culture-images GmbH/AL; 119 (LO), Alfmaler/SS; 120, Martin Strmiska/AL; 121, Universal Pictures/Photofest; 122 (UP), prochym/AS; 122 (LO), Masa Ushioda/Blue Planet Archive; 122 (eyes), 2DAssets/SS; 123 (toast), Alexstar/Dreamstime; 123 (CTR), Roberto Nistri/AL; 124-125 (UP), ramoncarretero/AS; 124-125 (LO), Elmiral/SS; 126 (pill), Ayseliani/AS; 126 (INSET), Jessica/AS; 127 (UP), SergeUWPhoto/SS; 127 (water), vchalup/AS; 127 (LO), timsimages/AS; 128, Timmothy Mcdade/SS; 129, Darin Sakdatorn/AS; 130, VladyslaV Travel photo/SS; 131, David B. Fleetham/Blue Planet Archive; 132-133, Franco Tempesta; 134, Matthew Oldfield, ScubaZoo/Science Source; 135, Alexey Vorobyov/AS; 136 (BACKGROUND), Darien Sanchez/AS; 136 (LO), prochym/AS; 137 (LE), happyvector071/AS; 137 (RT), Sabena Jane Blackbird/AL; 138, Barry Gaukel; 139 (UP), sam/AS; 139 (LO), Panda Vector/SS; 140, Andy Murch/Nature Picture Library; 141, topvectors/AS; 142 (UP), Willyam Bradberry/SS; 142 (CTR), murphy81/AS; 143, Cheryl-Samantha Owen/Nature Picture Library; 144-145, KW MacWilliams/Caters News Agency; 146, Uryadnikov Sergey/AS; 147 (UP), artjazz/SS; 147 (INSET), Janos/AS; 148, Drew/AS; 148 (flashlights), Moises Fernandez/SS; 148 (LO), Pavel Timofeev/AS; 149 (CTR LE), I. Pilon/SS; 149 (CTR RT), Werner Forman Archive/SS; 150, le bouil baptiste/SS; 151 (LO), viktorijareut/AS; 152-153, prochym/AS; 154 (UP), Shengyong Li/SS; 154 (LO RT), zimagine/AS; 154 (LO LE), Marta/AS; 155 (UP), Stephen Kajiura/Blue Planet Archive; 155 (LO LE), Anita Ponne/SS; 155 (stars), Foxyliam/SS; 156-157, Mohamad Haghani/Stocktrek Images/GI; 158 (UP), Alex Robinson/robertharding/AL; 158 (LO), Doug Perrine/AL; 159, David Fleetham/Nature Picture Library; 160, Stephen Frink/GI; 161 (LE), Jan Engel/AS; 161 (RT), Doug Perrine/Blue Planet Archive; 162 (UP), Andy Murch/Blue Planet Archive; 162 (LO), EreborMountain/SS; 163 (LE), Song_about_summer/AS; 164, Amos Nachoum/Blue Planet Archive; 165, Tom/AS; 166 (UP), Barbara Ash/SS; 166 (LO), popaukropa/AS; 167 (LE), Gerry Bishop/SS; 167 (UP RT), TextureMaster/AS; 168-169, kondratuk/AS; 170, Claudio Divizia/AS; 171 (UP), Alex Mustard/Nature Picture Library; 171 (LO), Viorel Sima/SS; 172, wildestanimal/GI; 173 (UP LE), TRAVELARIUM/AS; 173 (LO LE), Margaret/AS; 173 (RT), Don Smith/GI; 174 (UP), Doug Perrine/Blue Planet Archive; 174 (LO), Mark Conlin/Blue Planet Archive; 175 (shark), Tom/AS; 176 (LE), Jeff Gritchen/Digital First Media/Orange County Register via GI; 176 (RT), mix3r/AS; 177, Bernard Radvaner/GI; 178 (UP), FRANCOIS-XAVIER MARIT/AFP via GI; 178 (LO), Yuliia/AS; 179 (UP), Richard Graulich/The Palm Beach Post via Zuma Press; 179 (LO), Richard Peterson/SS; 178-179 (scale), gearstd/AS; 180, Efrain Padro/AL; 181, keltttt/AS; 182, Tom Haight/Blue Planet Archive; 183 (RT), Sterberg Museum of Natural History; 184 (sharks), Tom/AS; 184 (pencil), Pan Stock/SS; 184 (bus), Joy Brown/SS; 185, Sarah J. Mock; 186, Gil Cohiba/SS; 187 (LE), Hurst Photo/SS; 188 (UP), lunamarina/SS; 188 (LO LE), NG Maps; 190 (UP LE), Ronald C. Modra/GI; 190 (UP RT), mtsaride/AS; 190 (LO), LuisMiguel/AS; 191 (LE), Kharlamova/AS; 191 (CTR), Richard Ellis/Blue Planet Archive; 191 (UP RT), D-sign Studio 10/SS; 192, Viaval Tours/SS; 193 (LE), kilroy79/AS; 193 (CTR RT), archivector/AS; 194 (UP), guardiano007/SS; 194 (LO), David Gruber; 195, Skypixel/Dreamstime; 196 (UP), Zhanna/AS; 196 (LO), Samy Kassem/SS; 197, Jessie Pruitt/Buzzsaw Studio; 198, Warner Bros./Photofest; 199 (LE), Harry Collins/AS; 199 (crown), barks/AS; 199 (UP RT), dolimac/AS

HUNGRY FOR MORE SHARK STUFF?

NATIONAL GEOGRAPHIC KIDS

CAN'T GET ENOUGH Shark Stuff

FUN FACTS, AWESOME INFO, COOL GAMES, SILLY JOKES, AND MORE!

WE GET IT.

That's why we made ***Can't Get Enough Shark Stuff.*** It's the perfect combination of facts, stories, photos, and fun all about the world's most ferocious and fascinating ocean predator.

NATIONAL GEOGRAPHIC KIDS

AVAILABLE WHEREVER BOOKS ARE SOLD

Discover more at natgeokids.com

© 2022 National Geographic Partners, LLC